With Thee
Tender is the Night

John O'Brien OFM

Other books by the author

Catch the Wind
Return to Gethsemane
My one Friend is Darkness
Rachel's Tears and Mary's Song
Love rescue Me
Cry me a River
Therese and the Little Way of Love and Healing
Clare of Assisi: A living Flame of Love
Waiting for God: From trauma to Healing

For Walter Brueggemann
"Inspired and Inspiring"

Away! away! for I will fly to thee,
Not charioted by Bacchus and his parts,
But on the viewless wings of Poesy,
Though the dull brain perplexes and retards:
Already with thee! tender is the night,
And haply the Queen-Moon is on her throne,
Cluster'd around by all her starry Fays;
But here there is no light,
Save what from heaven is with the breezes blown
Through verdurous glooms and winding mossy ways.

(from John Keats, Ode to a Nightingale)

Contents

Abbreviations

CD: Karl Barth, Church Dogmatics (Edinburgh: 1956-1975)

GL: Hans Urs Von Balthasar, Theological Aesthetics (1982-1989)

LT: Letters of Thérèse

PG: Pagina Migne, Patrolgia Greca

PL: Pagina Migne, Patrologia Latina

TD: Hans Urs Von Balthasar, Theo-Drama: Theological Dramatic Theory (San Francisco: 1989-1998)

TL: Hans Urs Von Balthasar: Theologic (2000-2005)

Introduction

"I regard you as precious in my eyes and you are honoured and I love you" (Isa 43:4). This is what God says to his people in their pain, but is is also personal and through the prophets' words they reach us. In my life and I know in many others' lives this voice has been drowned out and replaced by other, more negative, voices. There is in many what is called an "inner chatterbox" that denies these words. Blaise Pascal said that many of our troubles begin because we cannot sit in a room alone for very long. We are afraid of the negative voices. In this work I invite the reader to pray the text, to hear the voice of God in place of the negative voices and make our hearts places of love.

John Keats (1795-1821) in 1819 knew he was very ill and he wrote his poem Ode to a Nightingale. The poem rejects the optimistic pursuit of pleasure found within Keats' earlier poems and it explores the themes of nature, transience and mortality. Keats' brother had died the year before and Keats knew himself to be ill. The Nightingale described within the poem is capable of living through its song. Keats lives on through his poetry. Keats begins the poem with:

> "My heart aches and a drowsy numbness pains
> My sense, as though of hemlock I had drunk"

One of the lines is "Tender is the night". F. Scott Fitzgerald (1891-1940) took the words "tender is the night" as the title of his 1934 book. This was semi-autobiographical. For him 'tender' means fragile, brittle and easily broken. He was suffering from alcoholism and his wife Zelda was in a mental institution. I take Keats' "tender is the night" and I say "With Thee Tender is the Night", meaning God. With him the night is not so lonely.

In 2015 Pope Francis announced an extraordinary Holy Year of Mercy (in 2016). He did this on Friday April 10th while celebrating a penitential service in St. Peter's Basilica. I see this as prophetic. So many have come to fear God, to feel unloved and unlovable. Pope

Francis said when he announced the Holy Year that the whole Church, which has much to receive mercy because we are sinners "will find the joy to rediscover and render fruitful the mercy of God, with which we are called to give consolation to every man and woman of our time."

The theme for the Holy Year is where Jesus says "be merciful as your father is merciful" (Lk 6:36). God's mercy is his compassion (misericordia). Jesus is the face of God's mercy. The perfection of God is in his merciful love. Compassion and mercy are the faces of love. Pope Francis reminds confessors that they should take Jesus' words to heart. Being harsh and cruel doesn't serve God's purposes. After Francis' announcement the Vatican released the Papal Bull "Misericordia Vultus (the Face of Mercy)", April 13th 2015[1]. Mercy is the foundation of the Church's life.

We are on a journey to discover the real face of God and allow his love to pardon, heal and transform us. In the same passage from Isaiah we read:

> "Do not be afraid, for I have redeemed you,
> I have called you by your name,
> You are mine."
> (Isa 43:1)

[1] The Jubilee is from December 8th 2015 to November 20th 2016.

Chapter One

The Darkness of God

How we think of God defines, in many ways, how we think of ourselves. Many have been brought up with the fear of Hell dominating their lives. In a certain style of preaching that many of us were subjected to, it seemed that unless there was a miracle it was impossible to be saved. Yet we were told God is love (1 John 4:8,16). Gustave Martelet wrote about Hell and the God of Love.[1] He says if God is love then Hell must be impossible, but then he points out that human beings are free. Love can be rejected. In this case hell, the utter rejection of love, can only exist for the person who is continually making a hell for himself. What interests me more about what Martelet says is what he says about the reaction of God to the rejection of love, and choosing the way of hatred. 'When God's love is rejected, it is as if a red-hot iron burns into his flesh, branding it forever... At this point, God's pain is as unfathomable as his love: faced with hell, our pain is only an echo of his.'[2] The hell of love refused impacts on the very heart of God. His suffering is the suffering of love. God suffers with us because of his infinite compassion and his suffering continues until the end of time. Yet this suffering is contained within his blessedness and he draws new life from suffering. We see this in the resurrection of Jesus.

Jean Galot looked at the pain of God.[3] In the sending of the word made flesh, Jesus, among us, he says the one who suffers is actually the Father who surrenders his son (p. 95). He accepts the offering of Jesus who surrenders himself as a sacrifice for humanity's sin. The son thus reveals the Father's suffering, and also he takes onto himself the full impact of sin, to offer himself in love.

[1] G. Martelet, L'au-delà Retrouvé, Christologie des fins dernières (Paris: 1974) p. 181-188.

[2] ibid, p. 188.

[3] J. Galot, Dieu souffre-t-il? (Paris: 1976)

Galot holds on firmly to the unchangeability of God's essence and his Covenant faithfulness (p. 155f). The divine persons, the Father (the one we call God), his son and the Holy Spirit created the world out of love. This love is what causes suffering. The pain of God is something unique to him and in his own mode of being. It is real suffering, but is located within the embrace of the divine joy (p. 150-153). His pain and our pain is overcome by love and the new creation is formed.

An Apathetic God

An idea that came down through the ages was that God somehow lived above everything and was unmoved. When this came into popular preaching God the Father became ever more remote. The "Father's" apatheia became in the minds of many an "apathetic God".

Von Balthasar looked at the idea of apatheia that the Fathers propounded so strongly.[4] The word apatheia means 'without pathos'. Pathos has different meanings and could signify many things.

It could be understood as some external misfortune, contrary to a person's will. This does not apply to God who freely chooses to suffer. Gregory Thaumaturgus (+270 A.D.) was a Christian bishop of the third century. He wrote "On the Inability and Ability of God to suffer" (TD5, p.219). Can God suffer if he so wishes? God can choose to suffer and, according to Gregory, since he suffers freely he is not subject to suffering but superior to it. According to Hilary of Poitiers, the incarnate one feels the pain bodily yet without suffering them; "he is surrendered, according to human nature, to the exposure of bodily matters, yet he is not touched by the harm of suffering" (De Trinitate, X, 24).

Pathos can be seen more sharply as having a connection with sin. Athanasius thought the sufferings, the pathé, invaded human nature as a result of the fall. We are delivered from sin by Christ's suffering in the flesh. According to Gregory of Nyssa real pathos "is a sickness of the

[4] H. Von Balthasar, Theodrama 5: The Last Act (Edinburgh: 1998) p. 218-223.

ability to choose". When Christ takes on himself, without sin or inclination to sin, is the healing of our fallenness from within; he touches our sickness in the way a doctor does. In the love of the Son we see the love of the Father (PG 45).

In this sense the 'pathē' are unruly passions that take away freedom. Augustine describes the passions (pathē) as a movement of the spirit against reason, although he admits anger and grief can serve moral purposes. God is not ruled by these passions; so he is impassible (PL 41, 242).

Origen attributes the pathos of pity to the eternal Son; if he had not felt pity for broken humanity he would not have allowed himself to come among us and suffer death. Origen says if the Son suffers then much more does the Father: "In his Providence he must suffer on account of man's suffering, just as the Son suffers our passions." (PG 13). If he suffers it is because of love.

So we see that the modern translation of 'apatheia' as apathetic does not do justice to what the Fathers meant by 'apatheia'. They were quick to find out that God is not ruled by passions (pathé) or strong emotions but because he loves he freely chooses suffering. In this sense we speak of the suffering of the 'impassible' God. In the modern period Bertrand R. Brasnett did write a work called "The Suffering of the Impassible God".[5] He emphasises God's loyalty to his covenant. Insofar as God's will for the world remains constant in the face of all vicissitudes and always hopes for the good, God may be called "impassible". However since God is profoundly engaged with his creation which continually resists him, makes him passible since he has handed himself over to his creation.

Karl Barth refines the approaches of Brasnett. He places Jesus Christ at the centre of God's covenant history with Israel and humankind. His death testifies to God's utter faithfulness to the Covenant, for in it God himself takes over the faithlessness of Israel and humankind: in it he

[5] B. Brasnett, The Suffering of the Impassible God (London 1928).

adopts their situation of complete lostness (CD, 11/2, p. 3-506). As the God of the Covenant and the Covenant partner, God in Christ endures the conflict in his own self (CD, 11/1, 412-22). Hence God's abandonment of Jesus is not only the central act of God's reconciliation with the world – which includes the revelation of creation's meaning and of its life of redemption. The crucified is the image of the invisible God (CD 11/2, 99) and hence, too, the image of God's 'passion' (CD IV/1, p. 164ff).

A Darkness Reserved to God Himself (TD5, p. 265ff)

God's goodness and love is not restricted by his power. His love reaches to infinity. His inaccessible light is beyond darkness and light as we know it, it follows that God's darkness is the aspect of his light we do not understand. This darkness is God's hidden suffering. God's infinite goodness is always against evil. This is the way to interpret God's wrathful judgements in the Old Testament. It is a picture of God's reaction to the contradiction of our sin. It is as it were the Father's 'Cross' that this picture of him must be unavoidable, until on the Cross the Son reveals his ultimate meaning.[6] On the Cross the Son "took all sin unto himself in such a way that God cannot strike the sinner without striking him".[7] So then God's anger is against evil and the Son has taken the evil of sin unto himself. St. Paul tells us "in Christ God was reconciling the world to himself." (2 Cor 5:19) and later he says "For our sake he made him to be sin who knew no sin, so that in him we might become the righteousness of God" (2 Cor 5:21).

Von Balthasar continues then to talk about Jesus' descent into Hell. Here he experienced the absence of God, a deep darkness and an infinite loneliness. Here the Son experiences the infinite pain of God who sees his love rejected. In the abandonment of Hell Jesus experiences the Father's darkness but not yet the Father. The dead Son "therefore accepts the mystery of the darkness just as the Father offers it to him: in

[6] A. Von Speyr, Isaias, p. 154f (cited in TD5, P. 266).

[7] Adrienne Von Speyr, Apokolypse (Johannes) (cited by Von Balthasar, TD5, p. 267).

the turning away of the Father himself." "He turns away from the Son in love, in order to allow him to share in his mystery."[8] The Son takes all the sin of the world unto himself and he feels the pain of dereliction and abandonment. Paradoxically this is when he is closest to the Father when he feels he is infinitely alone.

Von Balthasar puts this well. He says that the mystery of Good Friday and Holy Saturday is thus a mystery of the loneliness of love between Father and Son in the Spirit, so much so that the outcome of these events (in their reunion in the resurrection) which is a mystery of eternal life can take place only in full loneliness (TD5, p. 269).[9] In the end love wins over death, but as long as suffering lasts God continues, in his darkness, to suffer. We are called to be co-workers with Christ in bringing his dream of a redeemed world to reality. Jesus showed us that "greater love has no man than this, that a man lay down his life for his friends" (Jn 15:13). Jesus experienced suffering without any consolation, so that this suffering be transformed into heavenly joy. He wishes, with the co-operation of his brothers and sisters whom he has called, to spread this joy to all who suffer. As Péguy said in his poem "Le Porche du Mystère de la Deuxième Vertu",[10]

> "We must place our hope in God
> since he has placed his in us" (p. 603).

Mary is called Hope:

> "She who is only faith and love
> Because she is also hope made perfect" (p. 569).

Jesus seeks the one who has strayed and lays down his life for him.

> "... who almost forfeited himself
> He has unleashed fear and so has caused hope itself to well up
> In the very heart of God" (p. 571).

[8] Adrienne Von Speyr, John, The Birth of the Church (San Francisco: 1994) p. 155.

[9] Hans Von Balthasar cites Von Speyr, 4 John, p. 155.

[10] C. Péguy, Le Porche du Mystère de la Deuxième Vertu in Oeuvres Poétiques Complète (Paris: Gallimard, 1957) 527-670.

God had been seized with the anxiety of having to reject someone, yet Jesus in the power of the Spirit seeks out all who stray and extends his healing to a broken world. In this is hope, that all sorrow will be turned into joy (see Jn 16:20, Ap 11:7-13).

God is Love:

The psalms show the faith of the people in prayer. By reciting the psalm in the Temple, or in the synagogue, the psalmist makes an act of faith that when he utters the words, Yahweh (the name for God) is present to him and hears his prayer. Psalm 103 is a psalm in praise of God and his love. It praises God for his faithfulness, and is a meditation on God's mercy. In praying the psalm the people make an act of faith in this God.

Friedrich Nietzsche called this psalm "the psalm of Divine Justice". He criticised Christians who claimed that the God of the Old Testament was different from the God of the New, the God of Jesus Christ. No, it is the one God. St. Thérèse of Lisieux said that God's mercy is contained in his love and he knows our fragility. "Like a Father he is tender towards his children" (LT 226).[11] St. Angela of Foligno marveled at how the immensity of God could be concerned with her nothingness. Auguste Valensin spoke of God as a maternal father. He also said (echoing St. Thérèse) that the good God is more tender than a mother. He gave him (Valensin) his mercy and through this lens he sees the other attributes of God. He sees everything in God as love.[12]

Ps 103 is a hymn thanking God for his goodness. It is an act of faith in the mercy of God who loves us even when we think of ourselves as nothing. He is as much mother as father. Initially the psalmist recounts his personal history (v. 3-5) and he sees this in the context of God's covenant faithfulness (v. 6-7). This shows his generous compassion (8-10) and his liberality as Father (11-13). In the end God is all-loving and

[11] St. Thérèse of Lisieux, Letters of Thérèse, vol II (Washington: 1998), Feb 24, 1897, Loc. 6569.

[12] A. Valensin, La Joie dans la Foi (Paris: 1960), p. 32.

we are in his embrace. In the second Benediction, among the Jews, they address God as "You have loved us with an eternal love, our God: You have a great and superabundant pity for us, our Father, our king…"

"Bless the Lord, O my soul,
and all that is within me,
bless his holy name.
Bless the Lord, O my soul,
and do not forget all his benefits." (103: 1-2)

The psalmist calls on himself to praise God with all his being. He has received mercy from God and his whole being reverberates with thanksgiving.

The psalm continues:

"who forgives all your iniquity,
who heals all your diseases,
who redeems your life from the Pit,
who crowns you with steadfast
love and mercy,
who satisfies you with good as long as you live
so that your youth is renewed
like the eagle's." (103: 3-5)

It is God's way to forgive (cf Ps 25:11, 86:5, Am 7:2). In the ancient world a link was seen between sin and illness – though Job and 73 question the received wisdom of this. However there is a link between mind and body – our anxieties can make us ill. When the psalmist here is forgiven his youth is renewed like an eagle. In Is 40:31 we read, "Those who wait for the Lord shall renew their strength; they shall mount up with wings like eagles." In God the psalmist finds strength to face life and what it throws at him. God is a tender presence in the psalm.

Saint Augustine says that sin is a disease, but God heals us of all illness and diseases. We might think our sins are too big, but how much bigger is the all-powerful physician. We should abandon ourselves into his hands... he knows us and what we need (PL 37 Col 1319). When God enters into the heart of the one who prays he brings healing, mercy and love. The heart is renewed and the person becomes a "new creation".

> "The Lord works vindication
>   and justice for all who are oppressed.
> He made known his ways to Moses,
>   his acts to the people of Israel." (103: 6-7)

The Exodus continues in the mind of Israel as the great event that witnessed to the merciful way God looked after his people. It formed the basis for the continuing gratitude of Israel (cf Ps 78; 105). He did forgive the people when they strayed. Moses, who was disconsolate and weighed down by the burden of leadership, turns to God and says: "Show me your ways, so that I may know you and find favour in your sight." (Ex 33:13). The subsequent revelation to Moses leads into a statement about God's character: "The Lord, the Lord, a God merciful and gracious, slow to anger and abounding in steadfast love and faithfulness..." (Ex 34:6). This is the great statement of faith in the Old Testament. God's steadfast love is his hesed, his loving kindness to those he has called his own. His faithfulness (*emeth*) is his truth – he never changes his choice, even though those he has chosen reject him. His love is eternal. This leads us to the next section of the Psalm.

> "The Lord is merciful and gracious,
>   slow to anger and abounding in steadfast love.
> He will not always accuse,
>   nor will he keep his anger forever.
> He does not deal with us according to our sins,
>   nor repay us according to our iniquities." (103: 8-10)

The psalmist shows that the act of faith of Moses (Ex 34:6-7) is God's habitual way of dealing with his people. The pagan gods showed themselves to be changeable and spiteful, but not the God of Israel. He is infinitely patient with his people.

"For as the heavens are high above the earth,
so great is his steadfast love toward those who fear him;
as far as the east is from the west,
so far he removes our transgressions from us.
As a father has compassion for his children,
so the Lord has compassion for those who fear him."
(103: 11-13)

God's love and mercy are infinite. Isaiah uses the same language of a God who is compassionate and abundantly pardons. In Isa 55: 8-9, he declares "For my thoughts are not your thoughts, nor are your ways my ways, says the Lord. For as the heavens are higher than the earth, so are my ways higher than your ways and my thoughts than your thoughts." The psalmist gives us an image of a compassionate father with his child. In Isa 49:15, Isaiah uses the image of a mother caring for her child – even more does God care for his (her) children. The people of Israel are the children of God (see Exod 4:22; Deut 14:1; Isa 45:11).

God loves freely and gives all to those he cares about – even to giving his Son. He casts behind his back past failures (e.g. Isa 38:17; Mi 7:19). Paul Claudel calls Mary the "sacrament of the maternal goodness of God." By the power of the Holy Spirit she shares in his infinite compassion and radiates that compassion to those who come to know her. We can truly ask for what we need from such a God. In the parable of the Prodigal Son in the New Testament (Lk 15:11-32) we see how Jesus teaches us about the superabundant love of the Father.

"For he knows how we were made;
he remembers that we are dust." (103:14)

As creator God knows the origins of humankind (cf Gen 2:7; 3:9-19). He knows how fallible his creature is (cf Ps 90) and because of this he is generous in forgiveness (cf Ps 51). Charles de Foucauld in a letter to Madame de Bondy spoke of how one can never love enough, but God loves us more even than any mother could, since he is the one who formed us.[13]

[13] J.-F. Six, Itinéraire spirituel de Charles de Foucauld (Paris: 1983), p. 374f.

St. Thomas Aquinas sees in our misery one of the very reasons God has such compassion for us. In the New Testament Jesus calls this God, 'Abba', a term of intimacy and trust and we his disciples are called to call God 'Abba' (Gal 4:6, Rom 8:15, Mk 14:36).

> "As for mortals, their days are like grass;
> they flourish like a flower of the field;
> for the wind passes over it, and it is gone,
> and its place knows it no more.
> But the steadfast love of the Lord is from everlasting to everlasting
> on those who fear him,
> and his righteousness to children's children,
> to those who keep his covenant
> and remember to do his commandments." (103: 15-18)

God's pardon is not a sign of weakness, but a victory of his steadfast love (Ps 117:2). Man who is fickle and quickly perishes always has the infinite love of God. His love embraces all time (v. 17-18), space (v. 11-13) and reaches the whole universe (v. 19). He always has the human being before him (Ps 11:4). The *hesed*, the loving-kindness of God lasts for now and for-ever (e.g. Ps 113:2; 115:18; Isa 40:6-8, 59:21). He has made his covenant with his people. In the Gospel of John we read of those who keep his commandments "are those who love me; and those who love me will be loved by my Father, and I will love them and reveal myself to them." (Jn 14:21). Jesus' commandment is "that you love one another. Just as I have loved you, you also must love one another." (Jn 13:34). St. Paul says: "For the whole law is summed up in a single commandment 'You shall love your neighbour as yourself'" (Gal 5:14) and in Romans 13:10 he says "Love is the fulfilling of the Law." In the Magnificat we hear Mary say:

> "His mercy is for those who fear him
> from generation to generation." (Lk 1:50).

This infinite love confers on us a new dignity. The immensity of God's love breaks down the distance between us as creatures and God as God

and brings us into a loving communion in the Holy Spirit.
The psalm concludes:

> "The Lord has established his throne in the heavens,
> and his kingdom rules over all.
> Bless the Lord, O you his angels,
> you mighty ones who do his bidding,
> obedient to his spoken word.
> Bless the Lord, all his hosts,
> his ministers that do his will.
> Bless the Lord, all his works,
> in all places of his dominion.
> Bless the Lord, O my soul." (103: 19-22)

The Lord is God is an act of faith in God being ruler over all creation. Sometimes things appear otherwise – but as Julian of Norwich was assured: "All things will be well! and all manner of things will be well."[14] He is a God of compassion who reaches down to his people with his loving kindness (his *hesed*). All creation speaks his glory.

The final blessing of all the celestial court is based on the model of a royal blessing (see Job 1-2). In this praise the angels are called to praise God with all creation. As in Ps 19:2; 96: 11-13, Isa 6:3 all the dispersed people of God's world are called to share in the final blessing.

In the light of the Gospel of Jesus, Paul says "Bless those who persecute you: bless and do not curse." (Rom 12:14 cf Matt 5:44). The psalmist places his faith in the love and fidelity of God. Paul in his rethinking of his Jewish history says:

> "What then are we to say about these things? If God is for us, who is against us? He who did not withhold his own Son, but gave him up for all of us, will he not with him also give us everything else?" (Rom 8:31-33)

[14] Julian of Norwich, Revelation of Divine Love, chapter 31.

and later he says:

> "For I am convinced that neither death, nor life, nor angels, nor rulers, nor things present, nor things to come, nor powers, nor height, nor depth, nor anything else in all creation, will be able to separate us from the love of God in Christ Jesus our Lord." (Rom 8:38f).

Chapter 2

East of Eden

'East of Eden' is a novel by Nobel prize winner John Steinbeck, published in September 1952. East of Eden brings to life the intricate details of two families, the Trasks and the Hamiltons, and their interwoven stories. The book explores the themes of depravity, love and the struggle for acceptance and greatness, and the capacity for self-destruction and guilt and freedom. It binds these stories together with reference to and many parallels with the biblical 'Book of Genesis'. Two of the characters, Caleb and Aron, call to mind Cain and Abel of the Genesis story. Caleb is jealous of Aron and ultimately destroys him. Aron died after enlisting for World War I – but Caleb had shown him how lowly his mother had fallen and was a broken person. Aron was dead spiritually before his body died – a modern re-telling of Cain and Abel. Steinbeck took the title from a line in Genesis 4:16, "and Cain went out from the presence of the Lord and dwelt in the land of Nod, on the east of Eden" (King James version). The Book of Genesis in the early chapters (1-11) shows us how evil grew. East of Eden is a symbolic term which means we have left Paradise and we now dwell in a place that is far from Paradise. It symbolises the fallen state of humanity – we live in a place East of Eden.

Our world works hard and plays hard because people dare not stop lest in the stillness they might become overwhelmed by fears and anxieties. George Orwell wrote, in an essay called "Pleasure Spots":

> "The lights must never go out
> The music must always play
> Lest we should see what we are –
> Lost in a haunted wood,
> Children afraid of the dark
> Who have never been happy or good."

In our world of social media never have so many been so lonely. The rate of suicide among the young is alarming. Our fears and anxieties do catch up with us, no matter how hard we try to run.

In a sermon by Paul Tillich called "You are accepted" he made his definition of sin as estrangement or separation. We are far away from the source of love – we live very far East of Eden. Tillich described the human condition as separation from God, from self and from neighbour: Not only are we aware of our separation but many understand themselves as deserving this separation. We are unlovable and do not deserve love.[1] This is the temptation of so many. Bernanos spoke of how easy it is to hate oneself. In the face of this unloving the voice that says 'God is Love' seems to be remote – deep down many believe this might be true, but deep inside they do not feel this. They feel fear, anxiety and the feeling they are unloved and unlovable. Those who have suffered trauma and abuse know this place only too well. Yet people struggle on, battling with fear, self-loathing and doubt. Tillich describes grace coming to us as a wave of light breaking into our darkness, as if a voice were saying: "You are accepted, accepted by that which is greater than you and the name of which you do not know. Do not ask for the name now; perhaps you will find it later." (Essential Paul Tillich, p. 201).

The Courage to be:

> "We would rather be ruined than changed
> We would rather die in our dread
> Than climb the cross of the moment
> and let our illusions die."
>
> (W.H. Auden, The Age of Anxiety: A Baroque Eclogue)

The Age of Anxiety is a long poem written in six parts by Auden. It was first published in 1947 in the U.S. It deals with the quest to find identity in a shifting and increasingly industrialised world. It is set in a wartime bar in New York. Auden uses four characters – Quant, Malin, Rosetta

[1] Paul Tillich, The Essential Paul Tillich: An Anthology of the Writings of Paul Tillich (New York: 1987), p. 201.

and Emble – to explore and develop his themes. Towards the end of the war Auden joined the American forces (he lived during this period in New York). His job was to evaluate the impact of the American bombing on Germany. He found a bleak world. After the Nazis had been defeated there was a bleakness in the air and an all-encompassing anxiety and feeling of lostness. This inspired his work "Age of Anxiety". The poem won the Pulitzer Prize for Poetry in 1948 and it also inspired a symphony by composer Leonard Bernstein and also a ballet by Jerome Robbins. The lines quoted above show the loneliness and fear of being trapped in this bleakness. The feeling of bleakness was captured by T.S. Eliot in his poem "The Waste Land" written earlier. In theatre Tennessee Williams in such works as "The Glass Menagerie" and "A Streetcar Named Desire" showed the cruelty of the world towards the weak and vulnerable. Those who feel lost and alone in a hostile world know this place too well. Trauma, rejection, can make one feel unwanted, alone, unloved and the nagging feeling of being unlovable. It is the true loneliness of the modern age.

Paul Tillich, a German-born theologian, was aware of this world. He used Auden's "Age of Anxiety" to explore the theme of anxiety. Tillich was born in Germany in 1886 and became a Lutheran pastor. He served as a chaplain to the German army in World War I and was traumatized by his experiences in the trenches. It also showed him that we needed a theology and words in theology that had an impact on our lives. Tillich became professor of Theology at the University of Leipzig but when Hitler came to power he was dismissed from his post. Reinhold Niebuhr brought Tillich to America to New York city's 'Union Theological Seminary'. Part of Tillich's method was to say the Christian message must provide the answers implied in human existence. These answers are contained in the revelatory events on which Christianity is based (Systematic Theology II, p. 64). In 1952, The Courage to Be was published by Yale University Press. The book began as a set of lectures given by Tillich under the auspices of the Terry Foundation at Yale University.

Tillich uses Auden's "Age of Anxiety" to look at anxiety and courage. He distinguishes between anxiety and fear – fear has a definite object whereas anxiety faces such questions as guilt and condemnation, meaninglessness and death. In the face of anxiety Tillich looks at the idea of courage. He draws on philosophers like Plato, Aquinas, Nietzsche and Heidegger to understand courage. He says courage is the ability to affirm being in the face of non-being. Non-being is that which would destroy being. Through the different ages of anxiety people have had the courage to affirm being and life in the face of the threat of non-existence. He does not deny non-being but he does accept its possibility. In the act of faith one can be tempted to doubt, but one can still make the act of faith accepting the possibility or temptation to doubt. Denying doubt leads people to take fanatical positions. Tillich says that "courage is strength of mind, capable of conquering whatever threatens the attainment of the highest good" (p. 7). We must accept fear and anxiety but affirm life in the face of these – Tillich calls this taking "non-being" into "being".

In "The Courage to Be", Tillich describes how in self-affirmation we presuppose "participation in something which transcends itself" (165). Tillich speaks of God being on our side even when we are suffering and losing "To believe in love in the face of hatred, life in the face of death, day in the dark of night, good in the face of evil, all of these may seem to be hopelessly naive, wishful thinking, 'whistling in the dark'" – all of these to Tillich are manifestations of courage. It is the courage and confidence even to death, and "in spite of..." (168). Faith is of the same quality. It is the character of "accepting acceptance" (172). "The power of this self-affirmation is the power of being which is effective in every act of courage. Faith is the experience of this power" (172). Tillich speaks of the "God above God". By this he means that our categories cannot contain God. By naming him we do not contain him. He transcends our categories. He is greater than anything we can say about him (or her). If we say God is good, then his goodness far exceeds our idea of goodness. He is the very source of all that is good. He is the ground of our being. When Nietzsche rejected God it was a very narrow view of God that he rejected. This made way, says Tillich, for him to discuss "God above God". This "God above God" is the ultimate source of the courage to be.

We are grasped by the power of being itself. In mysticism the individual self strives for a participation in the ground of being. In the divine-human encounter we discover the courage to be. It is in the encounter that we know we are accepted in spite of the fear and doubt that is a real part of us. Even in the face of our guilt we can affirm ourselves as the accepted. "One could say that the courage to be is the courage to accept oneself in spite of being unacceptable." (p. 177). The acceptance of despair is on the boundary line of the courage to be. The act of faith doesn't remove doubt and despair – it accepts them, but affirms life "in spite of". "The courage to be is rooted in the God who appears when God has disappeared in the anxiety of doubt." (p. 190).

When we face our doubts and our near-despair then we allow God enter in. Neurosis occurs when we deny the negative parts of us or our experiences. Accepting acceptance is for many a difficult thing. The negative voices that result from trauma or long-term abuse or bullying can let the person believe that they are not worthy of acceptance or love. "All the structures of the self – the image of the body, the internalised images of others and ideals that lend a sense of coherence and purpose are invaded and systematically broken down."[2] The victim of an acute trauma may say that he or she are not themselves. The victim of a severe trauma may lose the sense that they have a self.

This is the reason Tillich speaks of courage. The temptation to despair for many can be great. Yet the act of faith and self-affirmation shows us that even in the midst of the darkness we hope. To accept acceptance is an act of courage in spite of the darkness that can surround us. Tillich brings out in a real way the statement of John in his first letter. There he says: "God is love; and those who abide in love abide in God and God abides in them" (1 Jn 4:16). We have our ideas of love but our love is imperfect. We imagine that God's love must be as imperfect as our love. He could not really love us. This is where Tillich's idea of 'God above God' is helpful because God is greater than and transcends our ideas of love. He loves absolutely and unconditionally. He accepts God loves us as we are. It is in the quiet moments of prayer that we can await the

[2] Judith Herman, Complex PTSD in Psychotraumatology (New York: 1995), p. 94f.

grace of truly knowing this. It is in the quiet moments we can let him in, "in spite of the voices" that tell us we are not worthy or that we are unlovable.

Jesus: The Sacrament of the Love of God:

God's will is that all people be saved (see 1 Tim 2:4). In the Gospel of John Jesus wishes that all come to eternal life. He prays, "this is eternal life that they know you, the only true God and Jesus Christ whom you have sent" (Jn 17:3). What is revealed in the Son is not a human ideal, but divine eternal life. Our world of time is contained within God's eternity, his eternal life. Jesus says: "I have come that they may have life and have it to the full" (Jn 10:10). The Spirit is the outflowing of this gift of life. His life tells of the Father's love for us – "The Father and I are one" (Jn 10:30). In him we see the acceptance and love of God made visible. By the power of the Holy Spirit Jesus overcame death and is present to us today to teach us this message.

In the discourse with Nicodemus Jesus says: "For God so loved the world that he gave his only son, so that everyone who believes in him may not perish but may have eternal life." Indeed, God did not send the Son into the world to condemn the world, but in order that the world might be saved through him (Jn 3:16f). In the Son we see that we are loved and accepted. We are forgiven. Jesus suffered, died and was raised to life with the Father by the power of the Spirit. He has called us to share in the relationship of love which is his with the Father. The Holy Spirit is the bond of this love and he brings us to share in this union of love.

John begins his Gospel with the prologue. Scholars argue as to whether he composed it or used an older hymn – but in the end the prologue finds a part in the Gospel and is significant for John's thought:

> "In the beginning was the Word, and the Word was with God, and the Word was God. He was in the beginning with God. All things came into being through him, and without him not one thing came into being. What has come into

> being in him was life, and the life was the light of all people. The light shines in the darkness, and the darkness did not overcome it.
>
> There was a man sent from God, whose name was John. He came as a witness to testify to the light, so that all might believe through him. He himself was not the light, but he came to testify to the light. The true light, which enlightens everyone, was coming into the world.
>
> He was in the world, and the world came into being through him; yet the world did not know him. He came to what was his own, and his own people did not accept him. But to all who received him, who believed in his name, he gave power to become children of God, who were born, not of blood or of the will of the flesh or of the will of man, but of God.
>
> And the Word became flesh and lived among us, and we have seen his glory, the glory as of a Father's only son, full of grace and truth." (Jn 1:1-14)

Jesus is the truth as the one sent by the Father. The declaration in the letter to the Colossians tells us: "In him the fullness of the deity dwells bodily and you have come to fullness in him who is the head of all rule and authority" (Col 2:9). In Ps 145:7ff we read that God is gracious, merciful, long suffering, full of kindness, compassionate, faithful and righteous. God now speaks his word (logos) to all creation. We read "in the beginning was the Word". The opening of John's Gospel is the same as the opening lines of the Book of Genesis. It refers to when there was no time – when creation was begun. God's Word created all things (v. 3). Logos translates the Hebrew word '*dabar*' and by Yahweh's *dabar* creation came to be. '*Dabar*' also refers to God's word communicated to human beings. God's word and guidance is called 'Torah'. In the New Testament in John 'logos' can also refer to Jesus' teaching to his disciples – ultimately his teaching is from the Father. His words bring life (see Jn 5:24 and 15:3). His words bring eternal life because he is the Word of God made flesh "… for the words you have given me, I have given to them and they have received them and know in truth I came from you" (Jn 17:8).

The Logos existed before creation. In the Wisdom literature (Prov 8:22-31; Sir 21:9, 24; Wisdom 8) God's wisdom is seen as the creative agent in the world. This is the wisdom that was close to God as Jesus explains he was (see Jn 17:5) and he came from God to bring salvation (see Jn 3:31ff), so that we might have eternal life (see Jn 8:14). Jesus is the embodied wisdom of God. The grace and truth of the Logos of God are personalised in Jesus. Origen says that the Word (logos) reveals the Father, because he knows the Father and can reveal him to those who cannot know the Father without a guide (PG 14:99ff) This is a mystery that can only be entered in silence and prayer. By the gift of the Spirit we can enter that union. In the Logos God sees all creation and all of us. We read 'all things came into being through him' (v. 3-4). In saying that the Word was God (v. 1) John goes beyond the Wisdom tradition and identifies the Logos with God.

We find a parallel in the Qumran documents to the prologue of John… "And by his knowledge all things came to be and by his thought he directs all that is, and without him not a thing is done." (1QS 11:11).

In v. 18 of the prologue we read "No one has ever seen God. It is God's only Son, who is close to the Father's heart, who has made him known." The Greek for close to the Father's heart is '*eis to kolpon*' (v. 18c). *Kolpos* can mean heart and shows the relationship of love between Son and the Father. Jesus came to lead us into that special relationship. In him the creation continues and the work of God will go on until the end of the world (see Jn 5:17; Ps 104:30).

In the Old Testament Wisdom was described as the primordial light, reflecting the eternal light of God (Wis 7:17). The Word embraces this light. Welcoming the light of God is to welcome his salvation. This light shone in the darkness and the darkness did not accept it. In Gen 1:24 God said let there be light and the light came to be. A new act of creation is taking place but there is opposition. John the Baptist testified to the light coming among us (Jn 1:6-10). The world did not accept Jesus.

The Logos is the light in its divine essence and this is the light that enlightens all. There were some who welcomed the light and these became children of God. In the Spirit they entered the love-relationship between the Son and the Father. This leads to the bold statement of the prologue: "...The Word became flesh and lived among us" (Jn 1:14). He goes on to emphasize that "we have seen his glory, the glory as of a Father's only Son, full of grace and truth." The Gospel grew from a witness account and reflection on the person of Jesus, the Word made flesh. The final aim of Jesus the Christ is to save all and lead the entire universe into God, to take us home from a land East of Eden. Jesus passed through death to resurrection. The resurrection is now life in God – he now lives in a sphere that is directed by the Holy Spirit. He is alive now to lead us into that union of love, directed by the Holy Spirit. In this is our hope.

Forever Young:

In the Gospel of Matthew we read: "Truly I tell you, unless you change and become like little children, you will never enter the Kingdom of Heaven" (Mtt 18:2) and "let the little children come to me for it is to such as these that the kingdom of heaven belongs" (Mtt 19:14). In all of us there is the "inner child" – that sensitive, vulnerable, needy part of ourselves. I was brought up (as were many) in which we were told to be strong and self-sufficient. We were taught to deny that "child" part of ourselves. Yet we cannot grow unless we accept all parts of ourselves – especially the unheeded part. Between us and God there is an infinite distance yet by love God has crossed over this divide and come to meet us – we see this in the Word made flesh. We can feel as if we are nothing, but in the eyes of love of God he doesn't see this. Auguste Valensin, in his work "La Joie dans la Foi", says God is more tender than any mother. He says he has received God's infinite mercy and through his mercy he has come to know God. He says: "My only love, Jesus, Eternal Word, for him your heart is maternal" (p. 32). St. Thérèse of Lisieux spoke of the tender love of God for his children (LT 226). She wished to know God and serve him but she admitted her smallness and saw in the figure of Jesus one would meet her in her smallness and lift her to the very heart of God. She used the image of an escalator to show this in her little way (Story of a Soul, MsC, 3r). In MsB she uses the image of an eagle lifting up the little bird towards the sun (MsB, 4v).

How do we enter the realm of love. In the end it is different for each one – but in the beginning it is good to have a place to start from. I use Ps 131 here. This is one of the so-called psalms of ascent. For us it is the coming to know God. In praying the psalm we realise that the psalm belongs in worship. When we pray the words we enter into a dialogue with God. We make an act of faith that he is present – even if for a time he seems silent. The words we use go straight to his heart and we await for him to hear and answer us. As much as we seek him he seeks us even more!

The image of God as mother is used here to let us know of God's tenderness. In Hosea we read:

> "Yet it was I taught Ephraim to walk.
> I took them up in my arms
> but they did not know that I healed them.
> I led them with cords of human kindness,
> with bands of love.
> I was to them like those
> who lift children to their cheeks.
> I bent down to them and fed them." (Hos 11:3f)

In the book of Isaiah we read:

> "As a mother comforts her child
> so I will comfort you;" (Isa 66:13)

This text was precious to Thérèse of Lisieux and she used it in the formulation of the 'Little Way'. In the Book of Consolation of Isaiah we had the following passage:

> "Can a woman forget her nursing child,
> or show no compassion for the children of her womb?
> Even if these forget,
> yet I will not forget you." (Is 49:15)

We can understand why John spoke of Jesus as close to the Father's heart (*eis to kolpon*). The Father has a maternal heart and Jesus shares this heart with him. In the New Testament we see Jesus have a special welcome for the little ones (see Mtt 19:13-15; Mk 10:13-16, Lk 18:15-17). Jesus is the full revelation of the tenderness of God (see Dei Verbum; 2-6).

The Hebrew word for tenderness is *rachamim*. It comes from the same root as *rehem* which means womb. This is how God's love is expressed. It is like the love of a mother for her child – yet God's tenderness is the source of all maternal love and is infinitely greater. By speaking of God (Yahweh) as mother we are being led into this mystery. We are awakened to consciousness and love by the smile of the mother when we are young. This smile of tenderness leads us to the infinite smile of love of God for us (see Von Balthasar, TD3, p. 175f). The smile of a mother awakens us to a Thou and leads us into the loving 'I - Thou' relationship with God. This prepares us to enter the text properly.

> "O Lord, my heart is not lifted up,
> my eyes are not raised too high;
> I do not occupy myself with things
> too great and too marvelous for me.
> But I have calmed and quieted my soul,
> like a weaned child with its mother;
> my soul is like the weaned child that is with me.
> O Israel, hope in the Lord
> from this time on and forevermore." (Ps 131)

Blaise Pascal once said that all the troubles of humanity arise because we do not know how to be silent and be at peace in our own room (Pensées; 136). In being silent we can hear the answer of God to our prayer. The psalm begins humbly. He has not gone after things too great; his trust is not in himself but in quiet and gentle trust. All his expectation is on God. He knows his own weakness and need of God. In the end God is in charge and not us. We can let God be God and we can become ourselves. St. John Chrysostom said that "humility is the beginning of prayer" (PG 55:30).

Then in verse 2 the psalmist gives himself into the hands of God. In being silent we can know we are loved and accepted.

> "The world is always upside-down, says God,
> and in a contrary sense.
> Happy those who can rest like a child
> And have like an infant who preserves
> that first Innocence."
>
> (C. Péguy, Le Mystère des Saints Innocents, p. 785)

The psalmist uses the image of God as mother. He is like a weaned child in its mother's arms. His "soul is like the weaned child that is within me." The image of the inner child has been used by psychology, as we saw. The image of God as mother is to be found in the Old Testament. God is greater than our conception of either mother or father. Auguste Valensin introduces yet another twist. He speaks of his joy when he was a child and the joy he experienced in the presence of his grandfather (La Joie dans la Foi, p. 141). God's love is the source and fount of all human love. All our human love is only a pale reflection of his infinite love – or to use the language of the psalm, 'of her infinite love'.

Dante fell in love with Beatrice when he was nine. This love stayed with him all his life. Later when he came to write his "Divina Commedia" Beatrice symbolised the love that would lead him to the heart of the Trinity who is love. Describing the purpose of the poem to his friend Can Grande he says:

> "... is to separate those living in this life from the state of misery and to lead them to the state of heavenly joy."[3]

In Paradiso (Paradise) the apostle James tells Dante he is to meet the God of love so that "you may strengthen in yourself and others the hope which rightly below enamors, say what it is and how your mind blossoms with it, and say whence it came to you" (Par 25:43-45). Dante had an experience of God's love and he wished to communicate this in

[3] see Joseph Anthony Mazzeo, The Letter to Can Grande della Scala in Mazzeo, Medieval Cultural Traditions in Dante's Comedy (Ithaca: 1960) p. 91-132.

his Comedy. In the Comedy we see the intreraction of love and desire in leading us to God. In the 'Inferno' Dante repents and is purified in the Purgatoria. He is now led into Paradiso where he will come into God's presence. Beatrice is his guide.

In canto 28 Dante gazes on God as the Prime mover, he says: "I saw a point which radiated a light so keen that the eye on which it blazes must close because of the great keenness" (28: 16-18). Then Beatrice and Dante enter the Empyrean, the dwelling place of God: "We have issued forth from the greatest body (the primum mobile) to the heaven which is pure light: light intellectual full of love, love of the good, full of joy, joy that transcends every sweetness" (30: 38-42). He is now raptured in divine light as Paul was at his conversion (Acts 22:6). Beatrice then leaves him to meet Mary, the virgin who brings him further on his path of love.

In the final canto Bernard of Clairvaux's famous prayer to the Virgin begins (Virgin Mother, daughter of thy son, humble and exalted more than any creature...) (33:1-3). Bernard begs Mary to grant Dante power so that he might see the vision of God. The conclusion of the Paradiso is a vision of God that is both trinitarian and Christological. "Within the profound and shining subsistence of the lofty light appeared to me three circles of three colours, and one magnitude; and one seemed reflected by the other, as rainbow by rainbow, and the third seemed fire breathed forth equally from the one and the other." (Canto 33:115-120). He perceives God as light. Dante says that the second of the three circles "seemed to me depicted with our own image on it" (33:131). This is a reference to the Word of God, the perfect image of the Father (Col 1:15-16). We are because he is. Then Dante is struck as if his mind was struck by a lightning flash in which its will came to it and he concludes the poem with the following lines:

> "Here power failed the lofty phantasy;
> but already my desire and my will were rolled,
> like a wheel that is evenly moved
> by the love that moves the sun and other stars."
>
> (33:142-145)

Edith Stein, too, spoke of the mystical experience of resting in God's presence. There is a state of rest in God, in which all activity of the spirit ceases, in which one can do nothing. One must abandon oneself totally to him.[4] In praying the psalm and then being silent we begin to hear that "silent music" that John of the Cross speaks. We are like the child that rests in its mother's arms – only now in an even greater love.

The psalmist concludes by calling on all Israel to hope in the Lord. In ancient Israel the time of weaning for a child was a time of great rejoicing for all the tribe (see Gen 1:28 and 1 Sam 1:20-23). Therefore all are called to hope. Simone Weil speaks of humanity and God coming to meet. They come to different places and one waits and waits. Both are impatient "Woe to the one who turns and goes away."[5] We have to wait in silence, but those who went before us like St. Thérèse, Dante, Edith Stein, inspire us that God will come in his own time and fill us with his love.

[4] Jean De Fabrègues, Edith Stein (New York: 1965) p. 48f.

[5] G. Ravasi, Il Libro Dei Salmi, (101-150) (Bologna: 1985), p. 661.

Chapter 3

Deep Calls to Deep

> "Dear sisters and brothers, the so-called world of adults may understand it, but we children don't. Why is it that countries which we call strong are so powerful in creating wars but are so weak in creating peace? Why is it that giving guns is so easy but giving books is so hard? Why is it that making tanks is so easy but building schools is so hard."
>
> (Malala Yousafzai, Nobel Lecture, 2014 Peace Prize)

Malala was shot by the Taliban in Pakistan but recovered. She is a campaigner for peace and education. She says education kills terrorism while guns kill terrorists. Giving the Nobel lecture she associated herself with Mother Teresa, Martin Luther King, Nelson Mandela and Aung San Suu Kyi. She says she is following in their footsteps. Her vision and compassion is global. She is a Muslim and is not ashamed to be associated with Christians like Mother Teresa and Martin Luther King. The word 'Malala' itself means sad or grief stricken but she points out that she, Malala, is happy. Her grandfather always took delight in his little 'Malala'. She has become joy. Her Nobel lecture begins:

Bismillah hir rahman ir rahim
In the name of God (Allah), the most merciful, the most beneficent.

Her question is telling. She uses the image of a child to confound the world of the so-called "adult". I remember once with Phil Vickery, who played for Wasps and England, we formed a mock front row (Rugby Union). Phil said I looked like a front-row forward. I said (in jest of course), "I didn't think I was that ugly!" Later on we discussed religion and the high principles contained within. We discussed the unconditional love of a child for its parents. We had been talking about the smile of love of his kids. Then came the stumbling block (skandalon in New Testament) – if all the religions preach such high ideals then why is there so much cruelty and innocent children suffer so much? Once again the world of the child confounded the world of the adult, this time the adult world of the major religions, including my own. Phil and I were left in silence – we had no answer.

Lack of Spirit:

These questions go to the nature of understanding evil. It is a topic that has teased the greatest minds – ultimately there is no answer. The people who make a difference are those who give their lives to alleviating the pain of others. It is often in looking at the opposite that we appreciate the spirit that moves these people.

Shoah is a 1985 French documentary, directed by Claude Lanzmann, about the Holocaust. The film primarily consists of interviews and visits to German Holocaust sites across Poland. A great number of people were interviewed. The documentary, monumentally long, was criticised for not talking about the many Poles who rescued Jews or to mention the millions of Poles who were killed by the Germans during the occupation of Poland. However, what the documentary does show is that so many people were involved in so many ways. They were those who manned the trains, the train-stations and were involved in some way in the process of bringing people to their deaths. None of these were guilty of murder, or would ever contemplate murder, yet they were caught up in the spirit of the time. It is a very grim documentary to watch.

'The Grapes of Wrath' is a realist novel written by John Steinbeck and published in 1939. The book is set during the Great Depression and focuses on the Joads, a poor family of tenant farmers driven from their Oklahoma home by drought, economic hardship, agricultural industry changes and bank foreclosures forcing tenant farmers out of work. Due to their hopeless situation, and in part because they are trapped in the 'Dust Bowl', the Joads set out for California.

It was Steinbeck's wife, Carol, who suggested the title. The title is a reference to the lyrics from "The Battle Hymn of the Republic", by Julia Ward Howe:

> "Mine eyes have seen the glory of the coming of the Lord:
> He is trampling out the vintage where the grapes of wrath
>   are stored:
> He hath loosed the fateful lightning of his terrible swift
>   sword:
> His truth is marching on."

These lyrics in turn refer to the Biblical passage from Revelation 14:19-20, an apocalyptic appeal to divine justice and deliverance from the oppression of judgement:

> "And the angel thrust his sickle in the earth, and gathered the vine of the earth, and cast it into the great winepress of the wrath of God..." (Rev 14:19f)

In chapter 25 of his book, Steinbeck says:

> "...and in the eyes of the hungry there is a growing wrath. In the souls of the people the grapes of wrath are filling and growing heavy, growing heavy for the vintage."
> (Grapes of Wrath, p. 533)

Steinbeck was angry at the people and events that created this distress and he confessed that he did his damnedest to rip the reader's nerves to rags.

In chapter 5, Steinbeck catches the way people get caught up in systems they cannot control. As the tenants have to leave the land they talk with the landowners:

> "The owners of the land came onto the land, or more often a spokesman for the owners came... Some of the owner men were kind because they hated what they had to do, and some of them were angry because they hated to be cruel, and some of them were cold... And all of them were caught in something larger than themselves... a bank or a finance company owned the land..." (Grapes of Wrath, p. 94)

In the Bible the forces that surround us are called the demons, the forces, the dominions. When we find ourselves in situations like the Joads we resort to the same language. We speak of the Spirit of the Age. We speak of confronting our demons. In the economic crash of the 2000's who was responsible? In the 1980's leaders spoke of the problem of regulation being regulation. It was presumed that the economic system would regulate itself. A passing knowledge of mathematical chaos theory would have alerted people as to how dangerous the de-regulation was. Chaos was introduced, due many times to deception and greed. The system crumbled! Like the landowners in Steinbeck's story, people were caught up in events and situations beyond their control. The banks did play a large part in the destruction of so many lives, but who in the banks were responsible? It was not the local manager or the teller one met. Yet one could speak of a spirit of banking that they were caught up in. Steinbeck describes the banks of the Depression in the following passage.

> "Yes the bank is only make of men. No, you're wrong there – quite wrong there. The bank is something else than men. It happens that every man in a bank hates what the bank does, and yet the bank does it. The bank is something more than men. It's the monster. Men made it, but they can't control it." (p. 96)

There is a spirit abroad – it is not individual but it affects our lives. Just as Malala pointed out there is no will for peace, so in our society there is a greed. To combat the spirit of the age we need another Spirit.

Karl Barth, when he was professor of theology at Gottingen in the 1920's, was given a present of Saint Thomas's 'Summa Theologiae'. He saw the need for a modern equivalent and began to write his monumental 'Church Dogmatics'. Towards the end of his life his thought turned towards the Holy Spirit, a theme he had left underdeveloped. He said he dreamed of a new theology which would begin with the third article of the creed, the Holy Spirit, the Lord and Giver of Life.[1] This points to a gap that was in Christian thought. There was a lot of talk and thought about Jesus, and the Father, but very little

[1] K. Barth, postscript to Schleirmacher-Auswahl, ed. H. Bolli (Munich: 1968), p. 310ff.

about the Holy Spirit. When we spoke of the Spirit of our age and the demons we had to face both in our private and public lives, there was no language or prayer-form for us to allow in the Spirit of God. If we are to heal, as individuals and as communities, we need to allow another Spirit to move us.

Towards a re-discovery of the Spirit:

The Spirit of our age is one in which money is God. Those who have money are admired, entrepreneurs are more admired than the person of faith who helps others. Status is marked by having more and more and despising those who have less and less. In this mix anger, resentment and violence are commonplace. There are many other powers in our world. There is intolerance and religious hatred. Love has been handed to the pornographers. The best selling items in the world are drugs and arms. In this mix speech of the Holy Spirit appears alien and foreign.

Yet the Spirit is irrepressible and the human spirit still longs for love. Sometimes we can feel that the negative events of life are things we should grow accustomed to, but we don't. In the Jewish and Christian traditions we find a strong hope that all that is negative will be changed. "God will wipe away every tear from their eyes, and death shall be no more, neither shall there be mourning nor crying nor pain any more." (Rev 21:4). We are told that loneliness will end. "...and he himself, God with them, shall be their God... and he who sat upon the throne said 'Behold I make all things new.'" (Rev 21:3-5). It is in the power of the Holy Spirit that Jesus overcame death, overcame hatred with love and lives now with the Father in the love of the Spirit. "Christ was crucified in weakness but lives in the power of God" (2 Cor 13:4). The weakness is his vulnerability and love, but this love proves greater than death. This power of God, the Holy Spirit is given to us. Just as Jesus was raised from the dead so we are promised the rebirth of everything living and the new creation of all things. We do not see this world yet, we still wait in hope in the in-between time of Jesus' resurrection and the final consummation of all times. Yet this hope continues to beat in our hearts and never goes away.

In the Book of Wisdom we read: "God's spirit fills the world and he who holds all things together knows every sound" (Wisdom 1:7). The possibility of perceiving God in all things and all things in God is grounded in the understanding of the Spirit of God as the power of creation and the wellspring of life. "The Spirit of God made me and the breath of the almighty has given me life." (Job 33:4).

In Ps 104 we read:

> "You turn your face away, they suffer,
> You stop their breath, they die
> and revert to dust.
> You give breath, fresh life returns
> You keep renewing the world."
>
> (Ps 104:29f)

It is the same spirit that inspired St. Francis in his Canticle of Creatures:

> "Most High, all-powerful, good Lord,
> all praise is yours, all glory, all honour,
> and all blessing.
> To you, alone, Most High, do they belong.
> No mortal lips are worthy to pronounce your name.
> All praise be yours, my Lord,
> through all you have made,
> and first my lord Brother Sun, who brings the day;
> and through whom you give us light.
> How beautiful is he, how radiant in all his splendour;
> Of you, Most High, he bears the likeness."

God is closer to us than we are to ourselves in love. God feels and experiences in his own way what we suffer. It is the way of eternal love, the way of the Spirit.

In the Old Testament the Hebrew word for spirit is '*ruach*'. It means God is a tempest, a storm, a force in body and soul. Ruach was probably an onomatopoeic word for a gale, such as the storm which divided the

Red Sea for Israel's exodus from Egypt (Ex 14:21). The word always means something living compared with something dead, something moving over against what is rigid and petrified.[2] In the transcendent sense it becomes the name for the irresistible force of the creator's power. Because people saw the livingness of life in the inhaling and exhaling of air, ruach was also the breath of life and the power to live enjoyed by all living creatures (Eccles. 12:7).

Yahweh's *ruach* and Yahweh's *dabar* (his word) are very close to one another. Ruach is thought of as the breath of God's voice. In Ps 33:6 we read: "By the word of the Lord the heavens were made and all his host by the *ruach* of his mouth". In Gen 1:2, God's spirit (*ruach*) hovered over the water. He forms the world from the primordial chaos.

In the Book of Judges, we read the account of the divine Spirit in Israel's charismatic leaders. Yahweh's ruach came upon Othniel (Judg 3:10), upon Gideon (6:34). Yahweh's ruach begins to stir Samson (13:25) and gave him great strength (14:6). After the Judges the spirit came to rest on the Kings. The spirit also inspired the prophets. The later prophets such as Amos, Hosea, Micah, Isaiah and Jeremiah proclaim God's word (dabar). The call to proclaim God's word takes place through the inspiration of the Holy Spirit. This is why we read in the prophet Amos: "I am no prophet, nor a prophet's son. I am a herdsman. But the Lord took me from following the flock and said to me, 'Go prophesy to my people Israel.' Now therefore hear the word of the Lord..." (Amos 7:14-16). When Saul is anointed king by the prophet Samuel (1 Sam 10), the king's endowment with the Spirit is ritualised in Israel. Nathan's prophecy to King David (2 Sam 7), gives Israel's monarchy a messianic perspective: "I will establish the throne of his kingdom for ever. I will be a father to him and he a son to me" (7:13f). In Ps 51 we hear of an individual, inward experience of the Spirit. We hear:

> "God create a clean heart in me,
> put into me a new and constant spirit,
> do not banish me from your presence,
> do not deprive me of your holy spirit." (Ps 51:10f)

[2] see J. Moltmann, The Spirit of Life: A Universal Affirmation (Minneapolis: 1994), p. 40f.

In the prophet Ezekiel (Ez 3:4) the prophet speaks of a new spirit and a new heart for all the people. What the psalms have to say about the presence of the Spirit in the depths of the human heart is developed by the Wisdom literature in the wider context of the Cosmos. In Proverbs 8, Job 28 and Ecclesiasticus the Wisdom of God is presented as an ordering power immanent in the world. As God's daughter Wisdom is described almost as an individual rejoicing in God's work. God's wisdom is poured out upon all his works (Eccles 1:9), it fills the whole world (Wis 1:7), for it is through Wisdom that God made all his works (Ps 104:24). In Wisdom he founded the earth (Prov 3:19). God's Wisdom speaks to human beings out of creation, so as to bring them into harmony with that creation, and in this way to make them wise. In the Book of Wisdom, Spirit and Wisdom (in Hebrew ruach and hokma) are very close to one another, they are interchangeable: "The Spirit of the Lord has filled all things" (1:7); "Thy immortal Spirit is in all things" (12:1); "I know everything that is hidden and manifest, for Wisdom the fashioner of all things, taught me. For in her there is a spirit that is intelligent..." (7:21f). There is a close link between spirit, word and wisdom. The Wisdom of God is expressed in his Word (especially his Word made flesh). The Spirit of God is the Spirit of this Wisdom.

The Presence:

The spirit (*ruach*) becomes the Holy Spirit in late Judaism. In early rabbinic literature, Holy Spirit means Spirit of the sanctuary (Moltmann, p. 47). It means a medium of revelation. The idea of God's dwelling among us is called the '*shekinah*'. The idea of the Shekinah developed out of cultic language. It originally meant God's tabernacle and his dwelling among his people. It meant the ark of the covenant and then God's presence in the Temple. Then after the destruction of the Temple came the idea of God dwelling with his people. The Shekinah shares Israel's joys and sufferings. The Shekinah is the presence of God himself. It is his special, willed and promised presence in the world. God's presence lifted "them (the people) up and carried them all the days of old" (Isa 63:9). He binds himself so close to Israel that he becomes of one heart and one soul with her. "In all their afflictions he was afflicted" (Isa 63:8f), "I am with him in trouble" (Ps 91:15). The idea of God suffering with and in his people was a source of consolation for Israel. Ps 23:4 speaks of the consoling presence of Yahweh with the psalmist in the valley of the shadow of death (Ps 23:4). God's presence will restore to glory when all is restored.

God loves his creation. God is bound to everyone in passionate affirmation (Moltmann, p. 50). By virtue of his love he has a supreme empathy with all that lives. When a creature turns away from this divine love, it becomes anxious, aggressive and destructive, because it becomes self-seeking. God is grieved and hurt, yet we always feel the call to be more authentic, we feel the need to be loved and accepted. When we can say 'thy will be done' we come to peace as does God; his shekinah is no longer in exile but returns to him. We get an intimation of God's joy when we find peace in him. These moments are rare but for all that they are real. In meeting other people we encounter those that God loves and whose presence is in them (his 'shekinah'). This helps us understand the saying of Jesus: "As you did this to one of the least of these my brethren, you did it to me" (Matt 25:40).

In the prophet Ezekiel the prophet is led by the Spirit to a vast valley where the bones of Israel's dead are lying. He hears the Lord's promise.

> "The hand of the Lord came upon me, and he brought me out by the spirit of the Lord and set me down in the middle of a valley; it was full of bones. He led me all around them; there were very many lying in the valley, and they were very dry. He said to me, "Mortal, can these bones live?" I answered, "O Lord God, you know." Then he said to me, "Prophesy to these bones, and say to them: O dry bones, hear the word of the Lord. Thus says the Lord God to these bones: I will cause breath to enter you, and you shall live. I will lay sinews on you, and will cause flesh to come upon you, and cover you with skin, and put breath in you, and you shall live; and you shall know that I am the Lord." So I prophesied as I had been commanded; and as I prophesied, suddenly there was a noise, a rattling, and the bones came

> together, bone to its bone. I looked, and there were sinews on them, and flesh had come upon them, and skin had covered them; but there was no breath in them. Then he said to me, "Prophesy to the breath, prophesy, mortal, and say to the breath: Thus says the Lord God: Come from the four winds, O breath, and breathe upon these slain, that they may live." I prophesied as he commanded me, and the breath came into them, and they lived, and stood on their feet, a vast multitude. Then he said to me, "Mortal, these bones are the whole house of Israel. They say, 'Our bones are dried up, and our hope is lost; we are cut off completely.' Therefore prophesy, and say to them, Thus says the Lord God: I am going to open your graves, and bring you up from your graves, O my people; and I will bring you back to the land of Israel. And you shall know that I am the Lord, when I open your graves, and bring you up from your graves, O my people. I will put my spirit within you, and you shall live, and I will place you on your own soil; then you shall know that I, the Lord, have spoken and will act," says the Lord." (Ez 37:1-14)

When God puts his Spirit into a people, his dwelling place will be among them. To be filled with the Spirit is God's shekinah. A new heart is placed among the people. The law is written in their hearts. As Ezekiel says:

> "A new heart I will give you and a new spirit (ruach) I will put within you, and I will take out of your flesh the heart of stone and give you a heart of flesh. And I will put my spirit (ruach) within you, and I will make you a people who walk in my statutes and are careful to observe my ordinances."
> (Ez 36:26f)

Jesus and the Spirit:

Israel's expectation of the Spirit was present in the ministry of John the Baptist who was filled with the Holy Spirit from his mother's womb (Lk 1:15,80). Consequently he was regarded by Jesus' disciples as the Elijah who was to come at the end-times (Matt 11:14). Jesus began his ministry soon after John. In the Gospel of John, John the Baptist recognises Jesus as the 'one to come', the one who comes after him who ranks before him and he goes on to say "I saw the Spirit coming down on him from heaven like a dove and resting on him" (Jn 1:30ff). In the Gospel of Matthew when Jesus is baptised by John we read, "...suddenly the heavens opened and he saw the Spirit descending ilke and dove and coming down on him. And a voice spoke from heaven 'This is my Son, the beloved, my favour rests on him.'" (Matt 3:16f). Jesus' ministry is in the Holy Spirit. He has come to reconcile us to God, to make us children of the Father: 'Think of the love that the Father has lavished on us, by letting us be called God's children; and that is what we are.' (1 Jn 3:1).

When we read of the Spirit resting on Jesus and the voice of God saying: 'You are my beloved son, with whom I am well pleased' (Mk 1:11), this refers to the call of the messiah, on whom, according to Is 61:1, the Spirit of God rests. It is in his special relationship with God the Father in the Holy Spirit that Jesus preaches. In the Spirit Jesus enters into the mutual history between himself and God the Father in whom through obedience (Heb 5:8) he will learn his role. The theme of the Spirit resting on him refers to the Shekinah. In the power of the Spirit Jesus drives out demons and heals the sick, he receives sinners and brings the kingdom of God to the poor. He is the spirit of love for the poor, the sick and the broken.

Jesus discovers his mission as he grows. He goes into the desert to find himself and he suffers temptations. Mark tells us that the Spirit drove Jesus to go into the desert (Mk 1:12). Even though Jesus heals he is not a superman above and beyond our suffering. According to Matt 8:17 he heals through his atoning representation. "He has borne our griefs and carried our sorrows" (Isa 53:4). The Spirit which accompanies Jesus is a sign of the new world to come where all find peace in God. In the letter to the Hebrews "Christ through the eternal Spirit offered himself without blemish to God" (Heb 9:14). When Jesus' death approached we see his agony in Gethsemane (Mk 14:32-42). Jesus cries out to God as 'Abba, Father'. By entering into his agony of death, and hell, he overcomes the division between the Father and us. In his resurrection, his overcoming of death in the power of the Holy Spirit, he enables us to call God 'Abba, Father' (see Gal 4:6; Rom 8:15). Love is stronger than death and this love is eternal, it remains (see Canticle 8:6, 1 Cor 13).

In the Acts of the Apostles the Apostles are fearful after Jesus has returned to the Father. They find themselves at Pentecost in prayer in union with Mary the mother of Jesus. Then suddenly they are filled with the Holy Spirit (Acts 2:1-13). They become the place where the Spirit dwells. Through the Spirit they discover the presence of God empowering them and they live from that place. They teach us we, too, can live in the Spirit and discover the God who is closer to us than we are to ourselves.

In the Gospel of John we read "If anyone loves me he will keep my word and my Father will love him and we shall come to him and make our home with him." (Jn 14:23). Jesus' command is that we love one another as he has loved us (Jn 13:34). We are not capable on our own of this love but God's Spirit is with us to teach us and in the Spirit the Father and Son live in us at the centre of our beings, in our hearts. When we pray silently we are led to share this living presence and allow ourselves to be loved. This is where we find healing. Healing does not mean our wounds go away, but it does mean they do not control our lives. Our life is in love with God – the Father and the Son live in us by the power of the Spirit. The Holy Spirit is the consoler, the paraclete and is the giver of life (Jn 3:6; 6:33). Jesus tells the disciples the Spirit will come after his death (Jn 16:8f), and he will be their helper (Jn 16:7-14). The Holy Spirit is the Spirit of eternal love between the Father and the Son and in the Spirit we share in the loving communion between Father and Son in the Holy Spirit. In this way we are led into the truth (see Jn 16:13).

In Acts 9:1-12 we read of Paul's coming to Jesus. He had been an oppressor of the new community and suddenly on the road to Damascus, a light from heaven comes and he is thrown to the ground. This is an event of God in the power of the Spirit. He hears a voice asking him

"Saul, Saul, why are you persecuting me?" He recognises the voice as that of Jesus who is present in the members of his community. This causes Paul to reassess his life and faith and re-interpret his life and Jewish heritage in the light of God being revealed in Jesus by the power of the Spirit.[3]

He writes about the Spirit in the first letter to the Corinthians. The Corinthians are divided among themselves and Paul wants them to centre their lives on Christ whose presence is mediated to them by the Spirit. In chapter 12 he speaks about the variety of gifts.

> "Now there are varieties of gifts, but the same Spirit; and there are varieties of services, but the same Lord; and there are varieties of activities, but it is the same God who activates all of them in everyone. To each is given the manifestation of the Spirit for the common good. To one is given through the Spirit the utterance of wisdom, and to another the utterance of knowledge according to the same Spirit, to another faith by the same Spirit, to another gifts of healing by the one Spirit, to another the working of miracles, to another prophecy, to another the discernment of spirits, to another various kinds of tongues, to another the interpretation of tongues. All these are activated by one and the same Spirit, who allots to each one individually just as the Spirit chooses."
>
> (1 Cor 12:4-11)

and later on he says:

> "Indeed, the body does not consist of one member but of many. If the foot would say, "Because I am not a hand, I do not belong to the body," that would not make it any less a part of the body. And if the ear would say, "Because I am not an eye, I do not belong to the body," that would not make it any less a part of the body. If the whole body were

[3] see N.T. Wright, Paul and the Faithfulness of God (London: 2013).

> an eye, where would the hearing be? If the whole body were hearing, where would the sense of smell be? But as it is, God arranged the members in the body, each one of them, as he chose. If all were a single member, where would the body be? As it is, there are many members, yet one body. The eye cannot say to the hand, "I have no need of you," nor again the head to the feet, "I have no need of you." On the contrary, the members of the body that seem to be weaker are indispensable, and those members of the body that we think less honorable we clothe with greater honor, and our less respectable members are treated with greater respect; whereas our more respectable members do not need this. But God has so arranged the body, giving the greater honor to the inferior member, that there may be no dissension within the body, but the members may have the same care for one another. If one member suffers, all suffer together with it; if one member is honored, all rejoice together with it."
>
> (1 Cor 12:14-26)

The gifts are given not for the glorification of the individual but are gifts of service to build one another up. He goes on to use the image of the body – no part however small or despised is unnecessary and one should not see our gifts as a source of pride but as a part of loving in the Holy Spirit. To cement his arguments on how important love is he has his beautiful hymn to love in 1 Cor 13. He says:

> "If I speak in the tongues of mortals and of angels, but do not have love, I am a noisy gong or a clanging cymbal. And if I have prophetic powers, and understand all mysteries and all knowledge, and if I have all faith, so as to remove mountains, but do not have love, I am nothing. If I give away all my possessions, and if I hand over my body so that I may boast, but do not have love, I gain nothing.
>
> Love is patient; love is kind; love is not envious or boastful or arrogant or rude. It does not insist on its own way; it is not irritable or resentful; it does not rejoice in wrongdoing,

but rejoices in the truth. It bears all things, believes all things, hopes all things, endures all things.
Love never ends. But as for prophecies, they will come to an end; as for tongues, they will cease; as for knowledge, it will come to an end. For we know only in part, and we prophesy only in part; but when the complete comes, the partial will come to an end. When I was a child, I spoke like a child, I thought like a child, I reasoned like a child; when I became an adult, I put an end to childish ways. For now we see in a mirror, dimly, but then we will see face to face. Now I know only in part; then I will know fully, even as I have been fully known. And now faith, hope, and love abide, these three; and the greatest of these is love."

(1 Cor 13:1-13)

The first verses of chapter 13 are well constructed. Speaking is related to the gift of tongues (1=12:8), faith (v.2=12:9), helping (v.3=12:28). Only by loving does the Christian exist authentically (1 Cor 1:30). The verbs used by Paul show how inadequate are Paul's and the Corinthians' efforts to love. It shows the need of the Holy Spirit. Seeing God face to face (see Exodus3:11; Num 12:8; Deut 34:10) means our union with God. Love is essential to this new life of union with God.

If I have not love I am nothing. He describes love as being never jealous, or boastful, or conceited. It is always ready to excuse, to trust, to hope and to endure. The Corinthians would know this is not what they practiced. Paul himself would have known he was not always kind or patient. It is a description of Jesus and he is the criterion of love. The Holy Spirit leads us into this love. This is what is important and is what lasts. We do not see this perfectly now. We are seeing a dim reflection in a mirror, but when we meet God we shall understand. It is love that remains, the greatest of the virtues and in love we shall know God and ourselves as he has loved us. This text was important for Thérèse of Lisieux and she placed it centre-stage in her Little Way. She said she would be love in the heart of the Church (MsB, 3V°) – it helped the recovery of a lost vision and in an age of fear led many to rediscover God as love. The Holy Spirit is love and this love is shown in the heart of Jesus. This is the centre of the Church – mercy, love and care. Thérèse led us to rediscover this heart.

Looking out for Love:

In chapter 5 of his letter to the Romans Paul speaks of our hope in sharing the glory of God (5:2). The glory of God is humanity that has been restored and healed and we are one with God. Paul speaks of lasting in his sufferings "knowing that suffering brings endurance, and endurance produces character, and character produces hope and hope does not disappoint us, because God's love for us has been poured into our hearts through the Holy Spirit that has been given us." (5:3-5) God pours his love into us no matter how broken, tender or brittle we feel. His love is constant. When we pray we long for this lover. St. Paul reminds us: "...the Spirit helps us in our weakness: for we do not know how to pray as we ought, but that very Spirit intercedes for us with sighs too deep for words. And God, who searches the heart, knows what is the mind of the Spirit, because the Spirit intercedes for the saints according to the will of God." (Rom 8:26-28). God's Spirit prays in us and is with us in our search for love. True love is found in God who reaches out to us with the Son, the Word made flesh and the Spirit.

Change comes from individuals or small groups of individuals. When we pray to enter God's love we open a space for ourselves to change and to help bring change in the society we live in. In the Kabbalah one of the words for God is makon, which means space. The Spirit fills that space with love and we find ourselves in that space. In Ps 42 we pray to God expressing our need of him and his love. In faith we know we are heard:

> "As a deer longs for flowing streams,
> so my soul longs for you, O God.
> My soul thirsts for God,
> for the living God.
> When shall I come and behold
> the face of God?
> My tears have been my food
> day and night,

while people say to me continually,
   "Where is your God?"
These things I remember,
   as I pour out my soul:
how I went with the throng,
   and led them in procession to the house of God,
with glad shouts and songs of thanksgiving,
   a multitude keeping festival.
Why are you cast down, O my soul,
   and why are you disquieted within me?
Hope in God; for I shall again praise him,
   my help and my God.
My soul is cast down within me;
   therefore I remember you
from the land of Jordan and of Hermon,
   from Mount Mizar.
Deep calls to deep
   at the thunder of your cataracts;
all your waves and your billows
   have gone over me.
By day the Lord commands his steadfast love,
   and at night his song is with me,
   a prayer to the God of my life.
I say to God, my rock,
   "Why have you forgotten me?
Why must I walk about mournfully
   because the enemy oppresses me?"
As with a deadly wound in my body,
   my adversaries taunt me,
while they say to me continually,
   "Where is your God?"
Why are you cast down, O my soul,
   and why are you disquieted within me?
Hope in God; for I shall again praise him,
   my help and my God."

(Ps 42:1-11)

Some see Ps 42 and 43 as forming one psalm. For our purposes I deal mainly with Ps 42. There is a moment between complaint and trust, with complaint finding expression in urgent questions – When? (42:2), Why? (42:5,9) and in the sarcastic comment of other people "Where is your God" (42:3). In our search for love these are the phases we often have to go through.

The psalm begins with an image from the desert. People and animals were often parched and were desperate for water to quench their thirst. This is the image used for our search for God. The image of the deer was common in the ancient near-east. We seek God with the same desire. The psalmist seeks God in the Temple. Seeing the face of God refers to being in his presence in the Temple (see Ps 11:7, 16:11, 17:15 etc.). Then he realises that this is in the past. He is filled with sadness because the Temple has been destroyed. The prophet Jeremiah says: "...there are no grapes on the vine, no figs on the fig tree; even the leaves are withered, and what I gave them has passed away from them." (Jer 8:14). Ps 102:9 says "For I eat ashes like bread and mingle tears with my drink." Our psalmist knows the pain of loss.

He recalls the days of praise (*Todah*) and worship and the great processions to the sanctuary (cf Ps 42:2-6; 107:27, Am 5:23, Ez 26:13). These give him hope even though his soul is cast down within him. The Hebrew word for soul is nephesh and this signifies his very interior, that which makes him what he is. He initiates a dialogue with his nephesh. Ps 62:2 says: "In God alone is my soul (nephesh) at rest." This is what he longs for. In Ps 116:7 we read: "Return my soul to your rest, for the Lord has dealt bountifully with you." In the midst of his confusion he comes back to his true peace in the love that is God. In this is his hope.

He uses the image of "deep calling to deep" to express his need. The image of deep refers to chaos. Out of his confusion he reaches out calling on God in the confusion. He longs to be made new. He recalls the time God offered on the great mountain to lead his people – Hermon and Jordan. He has to battle with the apparent silence or absence of God in his present situation. Yet he knows God works even when all appears to be night (see Ps 30:6). He does to heed the sarcasm of those who mock him because of the apparent absence of God (v.4). All faith finds its natural expression in worship. Through worship and prayer we open our hearts to God. This worship finds fulfillment in God's presence. The words of the psalm prayer lead us to him and there we find a heart filled with love. All is grace.

For completeness I include a brief look at Ps 43. Ps 42 is a lament in which the psalmist is in dialogue with himself. Ps 43 contains a prayer for God's intervention. Ps 42-43 are often taken as one. The psalm begins with the language of the law court (see Psalm 36) as the psalmist pleads for God to be both judge and defense counsel against an ungodly people who do not belong to the faithful (see Ps 4:3). God is the rock in whom the psalmist takes strength (see Ps 27:1). He is now battered in the dark chaos of despair and his sole hope is God leading him out of darkness into his light (Ps 27:1). He speaks of how he will go and praise God who hears him. In bringing his distress in prayer and worship to God he is confident he is heard. Indeed his faith is vindicated and he finds peace. He lives in faith and life and this sustains him.

> Judge me, God, defend my cause
> against a people who have no faithful love;
> from those who are treacherous and unjust,
> rescue me.
>
> For you are the God of my strength;
> why abandon me?
> Why must I go around in mourning,
> harassed by the enemy?
>
> Send out your light and your truth;
> they shall be my guide,
> to lead me to your holy mountain
> to the place where you dwell.
>
> Then I shall go to the altar of God,
> to the God of my joy.
> I will rejoice and praise you on the harp,
> O God, my God.

Why so downcast,
why all these sighs?
Hope in God! I will praise him still,
my Saviour, my God.

(Ps 43:1-5)

Chapter 4

The Scream

One of most famous paintings in the world is Edvard Munch's "The Scream". In Munch's diary of 22 January, 1892, he recorded the inspiration for the Scream:

> "I was walking along the road with two friends – the sun went down – I felt a gust of melancholy – suddenly the sky turned a bloody red. I stopped, leaned against the railing, tired to death – as the flaming skies hung like blood and sword over the blue-black fjord and the city – my friends went on – I stood there trembling with anxiety – and I felt a vast infinite scream through nature."

In 1892 Munch had painted a picture called "Sick Mood at Sunset, Despair". The picture catches the mood of ferocious existential anguish. This prefigures the Scream of 1893.

The Scream takes place beneath a boiling sky, aflame with yellow, orange and red. Below is a figure standing on a bridge. Wearing a sinuous blue coat, which appears to flow in a surreal way into a torrent of aqua, indigo and ultramarine behind him, he holds up two elongated hands on either side of his hairless, skull-like head. His eyes are wide with shock and he unleashes a bloodcurdling shriek. Despite distant vestiges of normality – two figures upon the bridge, a boat on the fjord – everything is suffused with a sense of primal, overwhelming horror. Munch actually made four versions of the "Scream" – the first in 1893.

Munch was born in 1868 to an impoverished military doctor and died in 1944. His work heavily influenced the avant-garde Expressionist movement that emerged in Germany and Austria in the early years of the 20th century. Munch also influenced Francis Bacon's pictures of howling popes. In 1984 Andy Warhol made a series of screen-prints that recast

"The Scream" in bright, eye-popping colours. The Scream is also a favourite of Tracey Emin. In 1998 she made a film in which she visited a Norwegian fjord and screamed for a full minute, while the camera lingered over the water. It also influenced film-maker Wes Craven where killers in "Scream" wore ghost-face masks inspired by Munch's painting.

The Old Order is threatened – Expressionism and an expressionist theologian:

In science Max Planck (1859-1947) had discovered the quantum effect and in 1905 Albert Einstein (1879-1955) presented a scientific understanding of nature without an absolute frame of reference and laid the basis for a new understanding of space and time. It was the subsequent development of quantum theory in 1924 and 1927 by Niels Bohr and Werner Heisenberg that led to the questioning of the classical world view of physics. Paul Dirac (1902-1984) postulated the existence of anti-matter which was discovered by Carl David Anderson in 1932. Louis de Broglie (1892-1987) showed the wave nature of matter in an equation and the idea of wave-particle duality was alive in physics.

In music, too, there was a free style of music. Notable musicians of this period were Arnold Shoenberg, Anton Webern and Alban Berg. There were also the figures of Bela Bartok, Igor Stravinsky and Paul Hindemith. Schoenberg and his students from 1908-1909 shattered seven-tone music as radically as Einstein's theory of relativity and later quantum theory shattered classical physics. There was an enormous scandal over a concert by the Schoenberg school in 1912. There were riots in Paris at the premiere of Stravinsky's 'Rite of Spring', which later became famous. Stravinsky called the Rite of Spring musical poetry. All the time Stravinsky was stamped by the influence of Catholicism and he hated to neglect morning Mass and the concept of God was all-embracing for him. Stravinsky lived from 1882-1971.

In his essay 'Concerning the Spiritual in Art' (1907) Wassily Kandinsky (1886-1944) had reduced doubt in the validity of the visible. "Every man who steeps himself in the spiritual possibilities of his art is a valuable helper in the building of the spiritual pyramid which will one day reach to heaven… In short, the working of the inner need and the development of art is an ever-advancing expression of the inner need..." (Concerning the Spiritual in Art (New York: 1977), p. 20-34). Colour and field of force took the place of objective, geometrical patterns.

Paul Klee (1879-1940) was in search of the objective, thus surpassing that which was naturalistic and superficial. He saw art as being pent with the act of creation generally:

> "Art is like creation and is true on the first and the last… My love is remote and religious. All that is Faustian is remote from me. I occupy a more distant, original part of creation where I presuppose formulae for human beings, animals, plants, stone and earth, fire, water, air and all the circling powers at the same time – Art is a parable of creation. God too died and gives himself specifically by fortuitous stages in the present."
>
> (Paul Klee, Tagenbücher (Cologne: 1957) p. 353f).

Klee wanted to break through the surface of reality to the point of uncovering primal formulae and the roots of form.

Franz Marc (1880-1916) developed abstract forms under the influence of Kandinsky. We see through matter: "Matter is something which human beings at most still tolerate, but do not recognise". Marc was killed on 4th March 1916 at the battle of Verdun.

All these strands formed part of the Avant-garde movement known as Expressionism. For Paul Tillich the planes, lines and cubes of Expressionism took on 'mystical transcendence', because they abstained from motives and objects, because of the high degree of abstraction in their control. Here Tillich claimed there was evidence of breaking through the form of begin that rests in itself. What is portrayed is not a world beyond as in earlier art, but an inner expression of things through themselves into the beyond.[1]

[1] Paul Tillich, Die Religiöse der Gegenwart (1926) in Gesammelte Werke X (Stuttgart: 1968) p. 33.

All these works were part of the search for the final form, the origin. They were attempts to look beyond what we see to the inner reality of things. Theologians such as Rudolf Otto with his work 'The Idea of the Holy' sought to find the final form of religious experience and criticised the spirit of bourgeois society. There were many studies in this time of the origin of religions. There were many key phrases from Expressionism that entered the theological world, the rediscovery of the dimension of eternity, the rebirth of God, the non-objectifiability of religion, the synthesis of mathematics and depth-experience. There were doubts about the validity of the visible and the primal grounds of the human soul. The new brand of theologians wanted once more to speak of the eternal. Karl-Josef Kuschel[2] situates Karl Barth in this time and noted the use of metaphors which sounded expressionist in his commentary on Romans. Barth says:

> "Jesus as the Christ, the Messiah, is the end of History and can be comprehended only in paradox (Kierkegaard) as victor (Blumhardt), as primal history (Overbeck). As the Christ, Jesus is the plane which lies beyond our comprehension. The plane which is known to us, he intersects vertically from above. Within history, Jesus as the Christ can be understood only as a problem or myth. As the Christ he brings the world to the Father. But we who stand in the concrete world know nothing and are incapable of knowing anything of that other world."
>
> (Barth, Romans, p. 29f).

The ground of faith is Jesus being the Son of God, the resurrection reveals his true significance. The resurrection cannot be explained in our terms. It is an act of God.

After Barth's university training and a two year assistant ship in Geneva, Barth became the pastor of a congregation in the industrial village of Safenwil, Switzerland. His life was filled with the joys, conflicts and challenges of most village pastors. A significant change in his life

[2] Karl-Josef Kuschel, Born before All Time (London: 1992), p. 83ff. I am indebted to Kuschel's work for this section.

occurred in October 1914 when he discovered that 93 German intellectuals had signed a "horrible manifesto justifying the war policy of Kaiser Wilhelm II and among them were almost all his former German teachers. This event took place during the war of 1914-1918. To Barth this constituted an enormous betrayal. Not only did it express the hypocrisy of certain liberal Protestants, but it constituted a profound questioning of the entire liberal position that went back to Schleirmacher. Up to this his enthusiasm for Schleirmacher knew no bounds. Now all his certainties had been shaken. Barth found he did not have the words to touch the hearts of his people. He began a dialogue with Eduard Thurneysen who was pastor of a neighbouring village. They turned back to the Bible to discover what was written there. Barth discovered with new eyes the Letter to the Romans. He described this new period as the discovery of the "strange New World of the Bible". He was no longer reading it as he had been trained to do, but now with eyes open. He challenged the Enlightenment's "turn to the subject". Barth asserted: "It is not the right human thoughts about God that form the content of the Bible, but the right divine thoughts about men" (The Strange New World of the Bible, in 'The Word of God and the Word of Men', p. 43). For Barth God is the content of the Bible. Jesus reveals God and the Old Testament shows the religious world Jesus grew up in.

Barth rediscovered Paul. What was important for him were the words of Paul and the events to which they bore witness: "The task of understanding Paul verse by verse has been enough of an assault upon me and the whole of today's thought and sensibilities. But of course I wanted to understand, not misunderstand Paul."[3] The result of this research was the publication of his commentary on the Letter to the Romans, Der Römerbrief (1919) and an updated version in 1922. This caused a shock to the theological establishment at the time because this was not their way of doing things. It was like there reception among some of Stravinsky's 'Rite of Spring'.

The priority for Barth was the action of God in the history of Jesus Christ against all historical leveling out. It was a matter of

[3] This quote is found in Richard E. Burnett, Karl Barth's Theological Exegesis (Grand Rapids: 2004), p. 284.

understanding Christ as the "newness from above" which founds a new world, a counter reality in the light of which one can criticise the world and society. Jesus Christ is none other than the eternal God who is sent:

> "God sends him – from the realm of the eternal, unfilled, unknown world of the beginning and the end. Therefore... he is "begotten not made"... Therefore he is "born of the Virgin Mary" – that is, he is our protest against assigning eternity to any humanity or nature, or history which we can observe. Therefore he is "very God and very man" – that is he is the document by which the original, lost-but-recoverable union with God and man is guaranteed."
>
> (Romans, p. 277).

This work would be the starting point for Barth's quest to help find words to understand God in Jesus and his call to us. His journey to the Church Dogmatics began in 1924 when he was given a gift of Thomas Aquinas's Summa Theologica. He said "Does my journey really lead there, or will we suddenly break out backwards into the free prophecy we used to love" (Letter to Eduard Thurnysen, 1924). In 1930 he published a little book, one of his favourites "Anselm: Fides Quarens Intellectum" (Anselm: Faith seeking an understanding). This describes the quest of Barth – the content of revelation was God revealing himself and we were to try and understand what God was saying.

Barth wanted to bring joy to people via his search for understanding and leading people to the peace of God. Yet in 1947 he would say it was a joy 'over the abyss'. The joy came at the cost of the death and resurrection of Jesus and this was costly. This is seen in Barth's love of the music of Mozart (+1791). Mozart had been able to give musical shape to the peace of God which transcends all. In the light of the final victory of God Mozart "heard the harmony of creation to which the shadow also belongs but in which the shadow is not darkness, deficiency is not defeat, sadness cannot become despair, trouble cannot degenerate into tragedy, and infinite melancholy is not ultimately forced to claim undisputed sway. Thus the cheerfulness in this harmony is not without its limits. But the light shines all the more brightly because it breaks forth from the shadow. The sweetness is also bitter and cannot therefore cloy. Life does not fear death but knows it well." (CDIII. 3, p. 298). Mozart affirmed life in the face of the despair that was in Europe after the Lisbon earthquake.

Barth influenced future generations of theologians. There were those who were for him, those who disagreed with him and those who took their lead from him and followed their own way. In this way he helped renew the Church. One of the people he influenced was Hans Urs Von Balthasar (+1988). When Von Balthasar came to Basle to be a University chaplain he was in a sort of theological rut. Barth helped him overcome this moment.[4] Later in Basle Von Balthasar would lecture on Barth's writings. Barth would attend the lectures because he wanted to know what he actually wrote. Barth had a sense of humour – a true sign of grace.

The Crucified God:

Barth knew the pain of the world, the 'scream' but he affirmed life in the face of death. Another theologian who was influenced initially by Barth was Jürgen Moltmann. Having been born in 1926 Jürgen Moltmann was conscripted for war service in World War II. He experienced the collapse of Germany and he was a prisoner of war. Here in wretchedness, forsakenness and daily humiliation he had an experience of God. It was "an experience of God's presence in the dark night of the soul: You are there even in Hell. A well-meaning army chaplain had given me a New Testament... but then I became fascinated by the psalms (which were printed as an appendix) and especially Ps 38: "I am dumb and silent, I hold my peace to no avail: my distress grows worse. I have to devour my grief within myself..." They (the Psalms) opened my eyes to the God who dwells among those who are of a broken heart" (Moltmann, Why I am a Christian, p. 8). He became a christian and studied theology, being influenced initially by Barth. He entered into dialogue with Ernest Bloch about hope.

[4] See podcast by Stephen D. Long and his book Saving Karl Barth: Hans Urs Von Balthasar's Preoccupation (Minneapolis: 2014)

Yet at the end of the sixties things had become bleak. The early hopes of the decade were fading with the Vietnam war, race riots, student protests, the Russian invasion of Czechoslovakia and the murders of Martin Luther King and Robert Kennedy. This led ultimately to Moltmann's 1972 book 'The Crucified God'. He called the crucifixion the special feature and the stumbling block of Christianity:

> "It is the crucified Christ on Golgotha who stands at the centre of faith, the Church and Christianity. What is really Christian can be recognised in the light of the Cross. At the same time the crucified Jesus is himself the most stringent criticism of Christian superstition. The only idea of God – the only vision of hope – the only act that can be called Christian is the one that can endure before the face of the dying, forsaken Christ."
>
> (Why I am a Christian, p. 14).

This laid down a doctrine of God thought out in terms of the crucified Christ which Moltmann was to pursue further. It came to a provisional climax in the 1980 work 'The Trinity and the Kingdom of God'.

In 'The Crucified God' Moltmann says that God himself was involved in the suffering of Christ on the cross. It is the revelation of God's love. A God who cannot suffer is poorer than any men. "For a God who is incapable of suffering is a being who cannot be involved. Suffering and injustice do not affect him... But the one who cannot suffer cannot love either. So he is also a loveless being" (Crucified God, p. 222). Being affected by the beloved and therefore vulnerable to suffering is essential to what is best and most valuable in human love. Pathos is love's greatness. God's love is shown in the self-giving of Jesus on the cross (Trinity and Kingdom of God, p. 82f). Moltmann sees the atheism of protest as the only serious atheism because it rebels against human suffering (Crucified God, 221, 252). Moltmann seeks to understand God in a way which does not avoid the questions of Atheism. He finds this in 'a theology of the Cross which understands God as the suffering God in the suffering of Christ and which cries out with the godforsaken God "My God why have you forsaken me?" For this theology God and suffering are no longer contradictions, as in theism and atheism, but God's being is in suffering and the suffering is in God's being itself, because God is love" (Crucified God, p. 227). Jesus suffers on the Cross and the Father suffers the pain of loss. The Holy Spirit maintains the link between the two. Jesus accepts the cross because, as Moltmann says, it includes "both the question of human guilt and men's liberation from it, and also the question of human suffering and men's liberation from it" (Crucified God, p. 134). Jesus suffers so as to redeem us from suffering.

In Mark's Gospel Jesus cries out "My God, my God, why have you forsaken me" (Mk 15:34) and dies letting out a loud scream. The significance of Jesus' abandonment is his identification with the godless and the godforsaken in the depths of their abandonment. The Cross is an event in which Jesus makes all human suffering his own. Jesus suffers from the love which is the superabundance and overflowing of his being (The Kingdom of God, p. 23). It is also the moment of God's creative and redemptive activity. It is through participation that God liberates his creation for its participation in his ultimate victory (Kingdom of God, p. 59f). It can be said of the cross that suffering in suffering is the lack of love. The cross can be summed up by saying

> "that suffering is overcome by suffering and wounds are healed by wounds. For the suffering in suffering is the lack of love, and the wounds in wounds are the abandonment, and the powerlessness in pain is unbelief. And therefore the suffering of abandonment is overcome by the suffering of love, which is not afraid of what is sick and ugly, but accepts it and takes it to itself to heal it. Through his own abandonment by God, the crucified Christ brings God to those abandoned by God. Through his suffering he brings eternal life to those who are dying."
>
> (Crucified God, p. 46).

In his earlier work 'Theology of Hope' Moltmann spoke of the resurrection. In the resurrection Jesus comes to new life in God. Death is overcome. Paul says:

So if in Christ there is anything that will move you, any incentive in love, any fellowship in the Spirit, any warmth or sympathy -- I appeal to you, make my joy complete by being of a single mind, one in love, one in heart and one in mind. Nothing is to be done out of jealousy or vanity; instead, out of humility of mind everyone should give preference to others, everyone pursuing not selfish interests but those of others. Make your own the mind of Christ Jesus:

Who, being in the form of God,
did not count equality with God
something to be grasped.
But he emptied himself,
taking the form of a slave,
becoming as human beings are;
and being in every way like a human being,
he was humbler yet,
even to accepting death, death on a cross.
And for this God raised him high,
and gave him the name
which is above all other names;
so that all beings in the heavens,
on earth and in the underworld, s
hould bend the knee at the name of Jesus
and that every tongue should acknowledge
Jesus Christ as Lord,
to the glory of God the Father.

(Phil 2:1-11)

Jesus' condition was divine. This describes human dignity in Gen 1:26-29. Jesus is the perfect icon of God. He emptied himself. He is subject to death. It also calls to mind the suffering servant of Isaiah (Isa 52:13-53:12). The self-denying act of Christ is accepted by God. Jesus is raised from the dead and is now 'Lord'. This reflects the early Christian confession (e.g. 1 Cor 12:3; Rom 10:9). He now has universal lordship (1 Cor 3:21ff; Rom 14:9) to the glory of God the Father. Jesus is now glorified. Resurrection is not resuscitation of a corpse. It is new life in

God. The resurrected Jesus was seen by many Paul tells us. In 1 Cor 15 we read:

> "I want to make quite clear to you, brothers, what the message of the gospel that I preached to you is; you accepted it and took your stand on it, and you are saved by it, if you keep to the message I preached to you; otherwise your coming to believe was in vain. The tradition I handed on to you in the first place, a tradition which I had myself received, was that Christ died for our sins, in accordance with the scriptures, and that he was buried; and that on the third day, he was raised to life, in accordance with the scriptures; and that he appeared to Cephas; and later to the Twelve; and next he appeared to more than five hundred of the brothers at the same time, most of whom are still with us, though some have fallen asleep; then he appeared to James, and then to all the apostles. Last of all he appeared to me too, as though I was a child born abnormally."
>
> (1 Cor 15:1-8)

and at the end death itself is overcome and we come to new life in Christ

> "And after this perishable nature has put on imperishability and this mortal nature has put on immortality, then will the words of scripture come true: Death is swallowed up in victory. Death, where is your victory? Death, where is your sting? The sting of death is sin, and the power of sin comes from the Law. Thank God, then, for giving us the victory through Jesus Christ our Lord.
>
> So, my dear brothers, keep firm and immovable, always abounding in energy for the Lord's work, being sure that in the Lord none of your labours is wasted."
>
> (1 Cor 15:54-58)

The Spirit is the first installment in the process of transformation that is even now under way and this will climax in the transformed resurrected body (2 Cor 4:6-5:5). All our thinking about Jesus begins with his resurrection (Theology of Hope, p. 165f). We are called to share in this new life by the gift of the Holy Spirit. In 2 Corinthians Paul piles up the imagery of the Holy Spirit – conformed into Christ, anointed, sealed, and given the downpayment of the Spirit in their hearts (1:21ff). The word downpayment (in Greek 'arrabon') is the first installment of the new life promised by God which will come to its fulfillment when Jesus comes again. Moltmann wrote his 'Theology of Hope' to remind us of this hope.

Pain and Hope:

On the Cross Jesus takes all our pain into himself and carries it to God the Father in the Holy Spirit. The resurrection is our hope. Ps 88 expresses the pain we suffer in the in-between time. It is the psalm written by one in great pain, deep distress and anguish. In the site in Jerusalem which marks where Jesus was kept prisoner, St Pietro in Gallicantu, this is the psalm that one reads. The prison was an underground hole to which Jesus would have to be let down into. The last look he would have seen would have been the look of betrayal and shame in Peter's eyes.

The superscript identifies this as one of the psalms of Korah. According to the Book of Chronicles the sons of Korah were Levites who served as "guardians of the threshold of the tabernacle, as their ancestors had been in charge of the Lord, the guardians of the Entrance" (1 Chron 9:19). In Numbers 16 there is an account of Korah's challenge to the authority of Moses. In the superscript is added the information that it is a maskil of Heman the Ezrahite. In 1 Chron 6:33 Heman appears as one of the singers appointed by David to sing in the house of the Lord. In Chronicles 16:41f he is given a prominent place in the Jerusalem Temple Orchestra (1 Chron 15:71). He appears in Kings 4:31 in being part of Solomon's court. This is our introduction to the dark night of the soul the psalmist is going to endure.

> "Yahweh, God of my salvation,
> when I cry out to you in the night,

may my prayer reach your presence,
hear my cry for help."

(Ps 88:1-2)

In psalm 18:6 we read

"I called to Yahweh in my anguish
I cried for help to my God;
From his Temple he heard my voice,
my cry comes to his ears."

(Ps 18:6)

In Ps 88 there is no such reassurance. Thomas Mann who wrote in the time of Expressionism said: "My nature is such that doubt, even desperation, seems to be more human, more honest, more artistic than any dominant optimism." (Cosiderazioni di un apolicito in Ravasi; Il Libro dei Psalmi, II, p. 813). However, the psalmist hopes his pain will touch the heart of God.

"For I am filled with misery,
my life is on the brink of Sheol;
already numbered among those who sink into oblivion,
I am as one bereft of strength,
left alone among the dead,
like the slaughtered lying in the grave,
whom you remember no more,
cut off as they are from your protection.
You have plunged me to the bottom of the grave,
in the darkness, in the depths;
weighted down by your anger,
kept low by your waves."

(Ps 88:3-7)

'Sheol' is the underworld where the dead go and in the Old Testament world-view there was no life there. The psalmist feels overcome with sadness (Lam 3:30; Ps 65:5). His sadness has led them to this 'sheol', the grave. He feels even now he is one of the dead like those remembered no more (see Ps 28:1; 30:4; 143:7; Pro 1:12 etc.). He feels infinite loneliness. He feels he can no longer communicate with God or humans (see Ps 6:6; 30:10; 31:23). In the place of death the dead do not feel God's presence. In verse 6 the psalmist blames God for all that has come to pass. Unlike Ps 18:6 the psalmist here feels he is not heard:

> "You have deprived me of my friends,
> made me repulsive to them,
> imprisoned, with no escape;
> my eyes are worn out with suffering.
> I call to you, Yahweh, all day,
> I stretch out my hands to you.
>
> Do you work wonders for the dead,
> can shadows rise up to praise you?
> Do they speak in the grave of your faithful love,
> of your constancy in the place of perdition?
> Are your wonders known in the darkness,
> your saving justice in the land of oblivion?
>
> But, for my part, I cry to you, Yahweh,
> every morning my prayer comes before you;
> why, Yahweh, do you rebuff me,
> turn your face away from me?
>
> Wretched and close to death since childhood,
> I have borne your terrors – I am finished!
> Your anger has overwhelmed me,
> your terrors annihilated me.
>
> They flood around me all day long,
> close in on me all at once.
> You have deprived me of friends and companions,
> and all that I know is the dark."
>
> (Ps 88:8-18)

This part of the psalm is the song of loneliness of the psalmist. It is like the scream of Munch, the cry of Jesus as he died. On the 1973 album 'Dark Side of the Moon' Pink Floyd recorded a song called "The Great Gig in the Sky". It started with reflections on death but Pink Floyd decided to have a voice 'wail' or if you like scream in harmony to the song. They hired Clare Torry. The song becomes like a great wordless cry to heaven for comfort. It catches the mood of this part of Ps 88.

The psalmist has lost his friends. He is like Job who finds his brothers are far from him, those closest to him have become strangers (Job 19:13ff). He feels as if a wall surrounds him and cuts him off from human contact. Tears consume his eyes (Ps 6:7-8; 31:10; Lam 2:11; 3:48-51; 5:17; Job 17:7).

He feels the silence of the grave where God is silent. He raises his hands in prayer in the traditional manner (Ps 28:2; 44:1; 65:3 etc.) but to no avail. In this land which he calls 'Abbadon' he no longer feels the love of God. He hopes for the loving smile of comfort of God which would dispel the night (see Ps 5:4; 17:15; 30:6; 46:6; 90:14; 130:6; 148:8) but it never comes. All is darkness. Without the light of the face of God the sick one falls into a deep pit of darkness. Like Job under the weight of his pain he feels destroyed (Job 6:4; 20:25; 33:7; Ps 55:5). His mind is flooded with the demons of the mind and he feels drowned beneath their attacks.

The psalm ends in an extreme melancholy. He feels he has lost God. The psalm ends in the Jerusalem Bible version which I used with the words "all that I know is the dark". The translation used in the Prayer of the Church says "My one friend is darkness". This is the feeling of utter loneliness. It is the pain of so many who suffer in hospitals, those who suffer violence of whatever kind against their person. George Bernanos in his work 'Nouvelle Histoire de Mouchette' paints a picture of Mouchette, abandoned, lonely and alone who takes her life. Bernanos refused to call her death suicide – she reached out for the hand of love that was never extended to her. It is the prayer of all the Mouchettes of this world. It is the prayer of Jesus who takes all this pain into himself.

The psalter does not end with Ps 88. Like Jesus conquering death the Psalter ends with praise. Even the lonely pain of Ps 88 is under the grace of God. Like Jesus being raised from the dead by the Holy Spirit so all who pray the psalm are still held by the Holy Spirit. Robert Bresson (1908-2004) made a film based on Bernanos' novel 'Mouchette' (1967), but when Mouchette takes her life the sound of Monteverdi's Magnificat is heard; Mouchette is precious to God, but not to a hostile, uncaring world. Bresson saw that Mouchette is to be found everywhere – in prisons, concentration camps, torture-chambers and all victims of human brutality and indifference.

Ps 150 which concludes the psalter is a psalm of joyful praise. It is like Mozart and Barth's joy. It is a joy over the abyss. Our hope lies in God whose son Jesus conquered death and has brought us into peace with God. In the end times, when all will be in all, every tear will be wiped away, no more sorrow or misery – God will be with us in love, peace and light (Rev 21:1-6).

Ps 150 is the last of the psalms of praise which began with Ps 145. It begins and ends with the injunction "Praise the Lord, Alleluia". God's praise refers to his holy place where he dwells. God is to be praised for his mighty deeds in saving his people. The Temple orchestra is called to play its role in the praise of God. Everything that lives and breathes is called to praise God – because in the end he is the victor.

Ps 150 reads as follows:

> "Alleluia!
> Praise God in his holy place,
> praise him in the heavenly vault of his power,
> praise him for his might deeds,
> praise him for all his greatness.
>
> Praise him with fanfare of trumpet,
> praise him with harp and lyre,
> praise him with tambourines and dancing,
> praise him with strings and pipes,

praise him with the clamour of cymbals,
praise him with triumphant cymbals,
Let everything that breathes praise Yahweh.
Alleluia!"

(Ps 150:1-8)

Chapter 5

The Appalling Strangeness of the Mercy of God

Vladimir Soloviev was a famous Russian thinker of the 19th century, dying in 1900, the dawn of a new century. He was a philosopher, poet, pamphleteer and literary critic who played a significant role in the development of Russian philosophy and poetry. He was an ecumenist who longed for the unity of the churches. He saw the Protestant churches as being influenced by St. Paul. One recalls the Antioch incident where Paul openly challenged Peter (Gal 2:11-14) He saw the Orthodox churches as being influenced by St. John – the spiritual Gospel and the emphasis on the Holy Spirit. He saw the Latin Church as being influenced by Matthew and the Latin Church was the bearer of tradition. He saw the need for all the traditions to come together and mutually interact. He spoke of our quest for God. "The divine problem is the human problem, just as the human problem is the divine problem... Man is at the other extreme of the divine mystery. God needs men; God wishes that men and not God only, would be loved and loving" (see A. Sicari, Chiamati per nome, (Milan: 1979), p. 149). We are a need of God. Jesus who revealed the Father had a human heart and when this heart was broken he suffered. In this way we come to know God. Ps 63 speaks about our thirst for God and by extension God's thirst for us and our love. Gregory of Nazianzen (+390) spoke of God as thirsty for us and our happiness so that we could thirst for him (PG 36, 398).

Psalm of David When he was in the desert of Judah

> "God, you are my God, I pine for you;
> my heart thirsts for you,
> my body longs for you,
> as a land parched, dreary and waterless.
> Thus I have gazed on you in the sanctuary,
> seeing your power and your glory.

Better your faithful love than life itself;
my lips will praise you.
Thus I will bless you all my life,
in your name lift up my hands.
All my longings fulfilled as with fat and rich foods,
a song of joy on my lips and praise in my mouth.

On my bed when I think of you,
I muse on you in the watches of the night;
for you have always been my help;
in the shadow of your wings I rejoice;
my heart clings to you,
your right hand supports me.

May those who are hounding me to death
go down to the depths of the earth,
given over to the blade of the sword,
and left as food for jackals.
Then the king shall rejoice in God,
all who swear by him shall gain recognition,
for the mouths of liars shall be silenced."

(Ps 63:1-11)

The superscript of the psalm refers to David's time wandering in the desert of Judea (1 Sam 22-26). V 1-3 is the song of the thirst for God. This parallels what we saw in Ps 42-43. He seeks God like the lover seeks the Beloved in the Canticle of Canticles – "My beloved is mine and I am his" (Can 2:16). He finds himself dry as in a desert and longs to find God. He says that without God is like being in a dry desolate land without water. In the land of the Bible thirst and the burning up of the land by the sun were catastrophes (see Is 5:6 and Jer 14). In Ps 143:6 we read: "I stretch out my hands to you; My heart like a land thirsty for you". The Temple is where the Shekinah is, which is God's presence by means of his Spirit. There the psalmist hopes to behold God's glory and presence. The psalmist is saying that God's presence is necessary for him to live. Sergio Quinzio said that God's love is more important than life. This saying was inspired by this psalm in which the psalmist spoke of God's kindness (hesed) as being better than life. For the Hebrew people and the psalmist the blessing of God was of ultimate importance.

Verses 4-8 speak of his "hunger" for God. He wishes to praise God because he feels his prayer is answered. His praise is echoed in Ps 104:33 "I shall sing to Yahweh all my life, make music to my God as long as I live" (Ps 104:33). The raising of the arms in prayer is something that found its way into Christianity. "In every place then, I want the men to lift up their hands reverently in prayer, with no anger or argument" (1 Tim 2:8). The entire being of the psalmist is at peace and healed when he experiences the presence of God (see Ps 16:2; 17:15; 23;1). He uses the image of fat and abundance to express the overcoming of his "hunger" for God. These were images of wellbeing, hospitality and goodness in the Old Testament (Is 35:2; Jer 31:14 see also Lev 3:16-17, etc.). There is an interesting parallel to this in Ps 36 where we read:

> "So the children of Adam
> take refuge in the shadow of your wings.
> The feast on the bounty of your house,
> You let them drink from your delicious streams;
> in you is the source of life,
> by your light we see the light."
>
> (Ps 36:7-9)

The psalmist is longing for a loving encounter with God. In the world of Paul he is longing for what Paul calls the love of God to be "poured into our hearts by the Holy Spirit given us" (Rom 5:5). This longing for God is with the psalmist always even in the depths of the night, after a time for deep meditation and contemplation (see Ps 4:5; 16:7; 17:3; 77:7; 119:55). There in the night Yahweh instructs the heart (Ps 16:7). He surrenders all his being into the hands of God. T.S. Eliot says in the Four Quartets (Little Gidding, 1942)

> "Love is the unfamiliar name
> Behind the hands that wove
> The intolerable shirt of flame
> Which human power cannot remove
> We only live, only suspire
> Consumed by either fire or fire."

Whereas earlier he reminded us in "The Dry Salvages" that: "People change and smile, but the agony abides".

This helps us understand the last part of the Psalm. Often our thirst and hunger for all that is good can be attacked and derailed by experiences in life. Yet the faith of the psalmist is such that he can affirm that God will triumph over these. The psalmist desires this peace of God with all his might. Kahlil Gibran (+1931) said of God: "...in giving yourself, you give everything" (The Prophet (Milan: 1976), p. 81). It is this love that enables us to understand more clearly the mercy of God at the taking away of our sins.

We are often stopped in our search for God by a sense of guilt and failure. This is the hand that blocks out the light. We do not see because we think we cannot be forgiven. This was a theme that greatly interested the writer Graham Greene (1904-1991).

Once Greene had an audience with pope Paul VI. The Pope said he enjoyed The Power And The Glory, one of Greene's books. Greene quipped that he was surprised that the Pope would read this one. Why, asked the Pope. Greene explained that the book had been banned by the Vatican! Pope Paul smiled and said maybe some might not like what was in it, especially the alcoholic priest but Greene should continue.

Greene suffered from depression and knew the confusion that engendered in his life. His characters were fallible and made mistakes, but Greene always saw they were held by the mercy of God. One of Greene's earlier works "Brighton Rock" contains a small-time gangster called Pinky. He is a mean psychopath and is a killer. Rose is a gentle waitress but she could be a witness against Pinky, so Pinky charms her and marries her. Rose loves Pinky and refuses to betray him, but she now believes she is damned because she is now Pinky's accomplice.

Pinky is killed and Rose despairs. But she receives this reassurance: "You can't conceive my child nor can I or anyone the appalling...strangeness of the mercy of God...if he (Pinky) loved you... That shows there was some good in him" in the end perhaps Rose is Pinky's salvation. She is not far from God in her love of Pinky. Human love is a redemptive force in Greene's works. The characters are tempted to despair at their inadequate response to God and what they perceive as their unworthiness of his love. Yet there is above all this the 'appalling strangeness of the mercy of God'. When Greene was dying he was asked was he afraid. No, he said, because he knew that mercy of God, he knew the appalling strangeness of the mercy of God.

Charles de Foucauld (1858-1916)

Charles was a French Catholic religious and a priest who lived among the Tuareg in the Sahara desert. He was assassinated outside the shelter he had built for the poor among the Tuareg. The prophet Mohamed forbade the killing of a holy 'man of the book', called a marabout – so Charles' death affected both communities. He was beatified on 13 November 2005 by Pope Benedict XVI. Charles was born in Strasbourg to a wealthy Christian family. Both his parents died in 1864 and Charles was devastated by the experience. The children, Charles and Marie, were placed under the care of their uncle, Colonel de Morlet. Charles began to drift from the faith of his youth. After school he attended Saint-Cyr Military Academy. He was dismissed from here. He inherited money from his grandfather but lost it enjoying the good life. He joined the Cavalry regiment of the army. He was dismissed again! However when he heard his regiment was in danger he joined again and abandoned his dissolute ways and fought with his comrades.

In 1882, fascinated by North Africa, he discharged himself and went to explore North Africa. He disguised himself as the servant of a rabbi and he was very impressed with the humility and prayer of the Muslim people. His research was well-received.

In 1886 he returned to Paris and began to make friends again with his family, in particular with his cousin, Marie de Bondy. He felt a thirst and desire to know God, "God, if you exist, make yourself known to me." He had come to know Abbé Henri de Huvelin through Marie and driven by his thirst for God, he asked Abbé de Huvelin to show him God. The priest told him to go to confession and unburden himself. This he did and he found peace. Later he would write

> "It is love which should reconcile you in me,
> not distance from my children."

Eventually Charles lived among the Tuareg in Algeria. He spoke of a God who would welcome us all – Catholic, Protestant and Muslim. At an early stage of his life he had been nicknamed 'Piggy' because of his love for the good life. Now he became an ascetic. He felt called like St. Francis to follow the poor Christ. Once in 1907 when Charles was ill, the people he ministered to, the poor Tuareg, ministered to him. He was very ill and weak but the kindness and care of the Tuareg restored him. In 1914 the 'Great War' broke out. Charles was a victim of this war, dying in Tamanrasset in 1916, a place Charles had built to protect the Tuareg during the conflict.

This was the prayer of abandonment of Charles:

> Father,
> I abandon myself into your hands
> do with me what you will.
> Whatever you may do, I thank you,
> I am ready for all, I accept all.
>
> Let only your will be done in me
> and in all your creatures.
> I wish no more than this, O Lord.
> Into your hands I commit my soul:
> I offer it to you with the love of my heart,
> for I love you, Lord and so need to give myself,
> to surrender myself into your hands without reserve,
> and with boundless confidence,
> for you are my Father.

Charles' vision had been distorted by his sense of personal failure and lack of self worth. When he poured out his pain in confessing to Abbé Huvelin he felt unburdened and experienced that mercy that Greene spoke of.

"You are precious in my eyes and honoured and I have loved you" (Is 43:4)

These are the words of God to comfort his people. They reach out to all of us. God sent his Son so as we could be reconciled to him. "I mean God was in Christ reconciling the world to himself...." (2 Cor 5:19). By his life, death and resurrection he brought this about. He sent the Holy Spirit among us so that we could share this new life of the resurrection. We become a new creation in Christ: "So for everyone in Christ there is a new creation: the old order is gone and a new being is there to see. It is all God's work: he reconciled us to himself through Christ..." (2 Cor 5:17f).

In chapter 15 of the Gospel of Luke, Jesus teaches us about the compassionate love of God in the parable of the Prodigal Son. I prefer to call it the parable of the Lovesick Father. The chapter begins with the Scribes and Pharisees condemning Jesus for consorting with sinners and eating with them. Jesus answers with a series of parables, the lost sheep (15:4-7), the lost drachma (15:8-10) and finally the parable of the lovesick Father (15:11-32). The parable reads as follows:

> "There was a man who had two sons. The younger one said to his father, "Father, let me have the share of the estate that will come to me." So the father divided the property between them. A few days later, the younger son got together everything he had and left for a distant country where he squandered his money on a life of debauchery.
>
> When he had spent it all, that country experienced a severe famine, and now he began to feel the pinch; so he hired himself out to one of the local inhabitants who put him on his farm to feed the pigs. And he would willingly have filled himself with the husks the pigs were eating but no-one would let him have them. Then he came to his senses and said, "How many of my father's hired men have all the food they want and more, and here am I dying of hunger! I will leave this place and go to my father and say: Father I have sinned against heaven and against you. I no longer deserve to be called your son; treat me as one of your hired men." So he left the place and went back to his father.
>
> While he was still a long way off, his father saw him and was moved with pity. He ran to the boy, clasped him in his arms and kissed him. Then his son said, "Father I have sinned against heaven and against you. I no longer deserve to be called your son." But the father said to his servants, "Quick! Bring out the best robe and put it on him; put a ring on his finger and sandals on his feet! Bring the calf we have been fattening and kill it; we will celebrate by having a feast, because this son of mine was dead and has come back to life; he was lost and is found." And they began to celebrate.
>
> Now the elder son was out in the fields, and on his way back, as he drew near the house, he could hear music and dancing. Calling one of the servants he asked what it was all about. The

> servant told him, "Your brother has come, and your father has killed the calf we had been fattening because he has got him back safe and sound." He was angry then and refused to go in, and his father came out and began to urge him to go in but he retorted to his father, "All these years I have slaved for you and never once disobeyed any orders of yours, yet you never offered me so much as a kid to celebrate with my friends. But, for this son of yours, when he comes back after swallowing up your property – he and his loose women – you kill the calf we had been fattening."
> The father said, "My son, you are with me always and all I have is yours. But it was only right we should celebrate and rejoice, because your brother here was dead and has come to life; he was lost and is found."
>
> (Lk 15:11-32)

The parable begins with a young man, the younger of the two sons, who asks his father for the share of his inheritance. The is the same as saying to the Father – to me you are dead. The two son story is commonplace in the Bible (see Gen 25:27-34, 27:1-36) with Jacob and Esau. The son loses his money and tends pigs. This is the conduct of a gentile. He decides to return home. When he was a long way off the Father "saw him". Obviously this was a moment he had been praying for and hoping for, for a long time. He is overjoyed and throws a party. In Rembrandt's painting of the prodigal son we see the Father embrace the son – it is interesting to note that one hand is feminine and the other masculine. The Father embraces both fatherly and motherly features. The father's love overflows, but the elder son is jealous. Jesus meant this for the ears of those standing by. The Scribes and Pharisees did not share in Jesus' dining with what they called sinners. They were self-righteous and begrudging. There was no love in their hearts.

Miserere: Ps 51

The title 'Miserere' comes from the opening of Ps 51 where the psalmist cries out "my God have mercy on me". Charles de Foucauld said this psalm was very precious both for him and all Christians. When Charles was in the army he had a mistress called 'Mimi'. When he decided to re-enlist he dismissed Mimi. A woman pointed out to me that he seemed to have no regard for Mimi – he was still totally self-centered. The weight of his wrongdoing blocked his eyes from seeing God. He was as sick as his sickest secret. When he unburdened himself he felt the peace and love of God. In this context we see why he loved Ps 51 so much. Georges Roualt (+1958) painted a series of paintings during the First World War entitled 'Miserere' and explores the theme of human experience and suffering. Roualt belonged to the Expressionist movement of that time. He showed images of the suffering Christ and he intermingled Christ's suffering with the poor and suffering. In music there was the 'Miserere' of Bach modeled on the Stabat Mater of Pergolesi and there was the Miserere of Donizetti composed in 1820.

In the Bible we read in Isaiah who says "though your sins are like scarlet they shall become white as snow..." (Isa 1:18). The image of snow is used in Ps 51. There are three different words used for sin in Ps 51. There is 'hatta' which has the sense of missing the target. In Proverbs 19:2 we read: "where knowledge is wanting, zeal is not good: whoever goes too quickly stumbles." The second word for sin is 'awon' – this signifies a turning away from the proper road. It has the sense of not being in harmony with the divine will. This is the sin of the prodigal son who turns once again to the Father (Lk 15:13, 19f). In Coleridge's 'Rime of the Ancient Mariner', the mariner's mindless act of vandalism in killing the albatross disturbs the harmony of creation and engenders suffering for all. The mariner finds himself alone:

> "Alone, alone, all, all alone
> Alone on a wide wide sea!
> And never a saint took pity on
> My soul in agony."

The third word for sin is 'Pesa' which means the rebellion of a vassal against his king (2 Kgs 3:4-5) and is the revolt of human beings against God (Ex 21:8; Jer 3:20; Is 1:20, 50:5). Yet in Jesus' parable of the lost sheep (Lk 15:4-7 and Mtt 18:12-14) this is the one Jesus seeks out. Charles de Foucauld was keenly aware of the dignity of every human being and Jesus' care for them – even if they were despised and rejected. He had come to know himself and his weakness, so he had compassion on others.

There is also the symbolism of cleansing or canceling out the debt in the psalm. The word used here is 'mahah', which means wiping out a debt (see

Ex 32:32f; Num 5:23). There is a more poetic image of this canceling out in Is 44:22:

"I have dispelled your acts of revolt
like a cloud,
and your sins like a mist.
Come back to me,
for I have redeemed you." (Is 44:22)

Being made whole again in splendour is a theme in the psalm. The Book of Leviticus gives a list of the various groups that become unclean, lepers (Lev 13:14; 20:4), those who have contact with impure animals (Lev 11:33; 17:15), or contact with corpses (Lev 21:1-4; 22:4). There is a ritual to re-integrate these and other groups into the community. This is behind some of the symbolism in Ps 51.

The image of the hyssop stick is also found in the psalm. This was used in the expiation of a leper (lev 14:4-6) and in liturgies that celebrated the covenant with God (Ex 24:8). In the account of the Exodus there is a link between the blood of the lamb and the hyssop stick: "Then take a bunch of hyssop, dip it in the blood that is in the basin, and with the blood from the basin touch the lintel and the doorposts..." (Ex 12:22). The angel of death passed over these houses. According to Jn 19:29 Jesus is offered a drink on a hyssop branch and in the Letter to the Hebrews the author speaks of the blood of the covenant being sprinkled on the faithful (Heb 9:19ff).

For the choirmaster Of David When the prophet Nathan had come to him because he had gone to Bathsheba

Have mercy on me, O God, in your faithful love,
in your great tenderness wipe away my offences;
wash me clean from my guilt,
purify me from my sin.

For I am well aware of my offences,
my sin is constantly in mind.
Against you, you alone, I have sinned,
I have done what you see to be wrong,

that you may show your saving justice when you pass
sentence,
and your victory may appear when you give judgement,
remember, I was born guilty,
a sinner from the moment of conception.

But you delight in sincerity of heart,
and in secret you teach me wisdom.
Purify me with hyssop till I am clean,
wash me till I am whiter than snow.

Let me hear the sound of joy and gladness,
and the bones you have crushed will dance.
Turn away your face from my sins,
and wipe away all my guilt."

(Ps 51:1-9)

The superscript refers to David's adultery with Bathsheba and his repentance (2 Sam 7). This shows us that the heart of the psalm is the confession of sin. In Ex 34:6-7, there is the great confession of faith "Jahweh, Jahweh, God of mercy and kindness, rich in grace and fidelity, who keeps his people to a thousand generations, who pardons faults, transgressions and sins,..." In this God the psalmist trusts and confesses his sin. The psalmist can pray his relationship with God be restored.

The words for sin in the first verses are the words we saw above ('hattat' - 'pesa' - 'a'won') which mean sin, transgression and rebellion. The psalmist asks to be cleansed of the sin – the words used are 'mahah' which means cancel, 'kabas' – wash, and 'tahar' which means purify. So we have a rebellion against God pitted against the mercy of God. The psalmist knows his sin, his alone. He cries out 'Have mercy on me' (hanan). This is a cry that is much used in the psalter (e.g. Ps 4:2; 6:3; 25:7; 30:11 etc.). The word hanan can mean grace, the grace of forgiveness, the graciousness of a king towards his vassal. It is something freely given.

This grace is freely given because of God's loving kindness (hesed). The word hesed refers to God's fidelity to his covenant and his love for those he has called. In the psalms the word has the significance of God's filing the earth with his love (Ps 33:5; 119:64), it can come into the heart of man and repose in him (33:22; 86:13; 89:25; 117:2; 119:41). Here because of God's love the psalmist can pray his relationship with Yahweh can be restored. In the first book of Chronicles we read 'Yahweh is love' (1 Chr 3:20). This is taken up later in Qumran and in the first letter of St. John we read 'God is love' (1 Jn 4:8,16). It is to the God of faithful love (hesed) that the psalmist prays.

He then speaks of the great tenderness of God. The word for tenderness is 'rachamim'. It has the same Hebrew root as 'rehem' which means womb. It refers to innermost compassion of a mother for her child. In Isaiah we are told that even if a mother could forget her child God could not forget his loved ones (Is 49:15 cf 30:18). Jeremiah often uses the word to express God's tenderness and love (e.g. 12:15; 16:5; 30:18; 31:20; 33:26; 42:16) and Hosea, one of the great romantic prophets uses it (Hos 1:6-7; 2:3; 6:21-25; 14:4). In Ps 103 we read: "As a father has love for his sons, so Yahweh has love for those who believe in him" (Ps 103:13). Rachamim, the feminine emotion is the word used for love. God is here both male and female. In Pope St. John Paul's encyclical 'Dives in Misericordia' (Rich in Mercy) (no. 4, note 52) he speaks of the motherly love of God (rachamim). He speaks of the special link there is between mother and child. This is freely given. It speaks of the sentiments of goodness, tenderness, patience and understanding and the willingness to pardon. This motherly love when applied to God in the Old Testament is shown when God delivers his people from dangers, and is seen in his willingness to forgive. He quotes Hosea: "I shall cure them of their disloyalty, I shall love them with all my heart, for my anger has turned away from them" (Hos 14:5). In the face of man's rebellion God shows mercy.

This love and mercy are the reasons for God's pardoning, the love-sick father of the parable comes to mind. Mercy is the very essence of God. It is against this God that he psalmist has sinned. He knows his sin. In Ps 32:5 we read:

> "I made my sin known to you,
> I did not conceal my guilt,
> I said I shall confess my sin to the Lord
> and you, for your part, took away my guilt,
> forgave my sin.
>
> (Ps 32:5)

and in Ps 38 we read "… I made no secret of my guilt, I am anxious at the thought of my sin" (Ps 38:18). Savonarola spoke of feeling the immensity of his sin but being relieved by the thought of the mercy of God. The greatest evil is that in our own hearts, but God is greater than our hearts. When we sin against our brother or sister we sin against God. Charles de Foucauld spoke of seeing Jesus in every person: "Above all see Jesus in every person and consequently treat each one as an equal and as a brother or sister, but also with great humility, respect and selfless generosity." The other person is the brother or sister for whom Jesus died (1 Cor 8:11f).

In the great parable of the Last Judgement in Matthew's gospel we read:

> "When the Son of man comes in his glory, escorted by all the angels, then he will take his seat on his throne of glory. All nations will be assembled before him and he will separate people one from another as the shepherd separates sheep from goats. He will place the sheep on his right hand and the goats on his left. Then the King will say to those on his right hand, "Come, you whom my Father has blessed, take as your heritage the kingdom prepared for you since the foundation of the world. For I was hungry and you gave me food, I was thirsty and you gave me drink, I was a stranger and you made me welcome, lacking clothes and you clothed me, sick and you visited me, in prison and you came to see me." Then the upright will say to him in reply, "Lord, when did we see you hungry and feed you, or thirsty and give you drink? When did we see you a stranger and make you welcome, lacking clothes and clothe you? When did we find you sick or in prison and go to see you?" And the King will answer, "In truth I tell you, in so far as you did this to one of the least of these brothers of mine, you did it to me."
>
> (Matt 25:31-41)

Whatever we do to the least of our brothers and sisters we do to Jesus. Charles reminds us of this in his writings and life.

The psalmist recognises that God can justly judge him, but God's justice is his saving justice and is enfolded in his love. All of man's reality is typified by an alienation from God. We live far east of Eden. In the Book of Genesis we read “Man’s instincts are inclined towards evil from his youth” (Gen 8:21). In Job we read “how can a man justify himself before God and appear pure…” (Job 25:4). Later Paul will tell us: “What a wretched man I am! Who will rescue me from this body doomed to death? God – thanks be to him – through Jesus Christ our Lord” (Rom 7:24f). He, the psalmist, asks God to purify him. He speaks of being purified with hyssop (see Ex 12:22). In the Letter to the Hebrews we read: “In fact according to the Law practically every purification takes place by means of blood; and if there is no shedding of blood, there is no remission (Heb 9:19) and later we read “He (Jesus) on the other hand has offered one single sacrifice for sins, and then taken his place forever at the right hand of God, … By virtue of that one single offering he has achieved the eternal perfection of all who are sanctified (Heb 10:12ff). God was the one “who in and through Christ reconciled the world to himself” (2 Cor 5:19). God in Christ participates in human suffering and alienation and gives himself without reserve. He suffers alienation, mental and physical anguish, and death. On the Cross Jesus takes the estrangement, the meaninglessness and the despair of lostness into himself, but love is stronger than death. Jesus is brought back to life and by the power of the Spirit we are called to share in this new life.

There is a joy for the psalmist in being liberated from his burden:

> “At the sight your heart will rejoice,
> and your limbs regain vigour like the grass.” (Is 66:14)

We are as sick as our sickest secret, but once we come to terms with our darkness and God’s mercy our whole being is remedied (see Ps 6:3-9; 31:39; 32:2; 42:10; 102:4). In this sense we are a new creation (see Ez with the new life coming to the dead bones).

> “But you delight in sincerity of heart,
> and in secret you teach me wisdom.
> Purify me with hyssop till I am clean,
> wash me till I am whiter than snow.
>
> Let me hear the sound of joy and gladness,
> and the bones you have crushed will dance.
> Turn away your face from my sins,
> and wipe away all my guilt.

God, create in me a clean heart,
renew within me a resolute spirit,
do not thrust me away from your presence,
do not take away from me your spirit of holiness.

Give me back the joy of your salvation,
sustain in me a generous spirit.
I shall teach the wicked your paths,
and sinners will return to you.

Deliver me from bloodshed, God, God of my salvation,
and my tongue will acclaim your saving justice.
Lord, open my lips,
and my mouth will speak out your praise.

Sacrifice gives you no pleasure,
burnt offering you do not desire.
Sacrifice to God is a broken spirit,
a broken, contrite heart you never scorn.

(Ps 51:6-17)

The Talmud speaks of when precious vessels are broken it is only by means of fusion they can be brought back together again (Hagiga 15a). This idea is found in the part of Ps 51. Hymn XI, of Qumran speaks of God raising us from the dust to make us new. In the parable of the prodigal son we read how the young son was dead but is now raised to life (Lk 15:32). Charles de Foucauld had the same experience. The word for create is 'bara' the same word used for the creation of the world (Gen 1:1; Is 48:7; Ps 104:30; 148:5). The psalmist asks for a new heart to be created in him. It can mean both create or renew, restore (Gen 31:21; Is 48:7; 65:17). The word for the new covenant God makes is expressed by the term heart (Jer 24:7, 31:33, 32:39; Ez 36:25-27). The term heart refers to one's innermost being and can also symbolise one's spirit. This renewal by the Spirit of God is found in the investiture of Saul (1 Sam 10:9-10) and is poured out on David in his consecration (1 Sam 16:3) and is the same Spirit poured out on the messianic king (Is 11:1-2) and in the prophet Joel is poured out over all the people (Joel 3). The new covenant spoken of by Jeremiah and Ezekiel speaks of the creation of a new heart capable of knowing God (Jer 24:7) and this Spirit gives new life (Ez 36:26f). In our psalm the heart at one with God in reconciliation is a new creation. In the Gospel of John we read "Receive the Holy Spirit, whose sins you forgive they shall be forgiven" (Jn 20:22f). This is the same Spirit that hovered over the waters (Gen 1:2) and from the primordial chaos produced creation. Over the chaos of our being he produces new life. By this Spirit we are washed clean. He is the presence of God, the Shekinah, among us (see Ps 81:13). He is God's empowering presence. The psalmist prays for a renewed spirit of generosity so he shares his joy and healing. The Spirit who is over all creation is the one who renews us individually. The renewal of the sinner gives him new heart to proclaim to others the goodness of God. There is need for sacrifice (Ps 40:7; 69:32; Dt 3:38-40), but this is useless without a broken and contrite heart (Is 1:11-14; Hos 6:6; Am 5:21-27; Mi 6:6-8; Jer 6:20, 7:21-24 etc.).

> "In your graciousness do good to Zion,
> rebuild the walls of Jerusalem.
> Then you will delight in upright sacrifices,
> – burnt offerings and whole oblations –
> and young bulls will be offered on your altar."
>
> (Ps 51:18f)

The psalm ends with a call for God to bless all. When one is healed and finds peace, many are healed. St. Seraphim of Sarov said the aim of the Christian life is to receive the Holy Spirit. This is the prayer of Ps 51, a prayer for a new beginning, a new heart and in the healing God draws in many others.

Chapter 6

The Terrified Children of the Waste Land

> "You who live secure in your lukewarm homes, you who come home in the evening to a warm meal, and the faces of friends: Consider is this man a human, the one who works in mud, who knows no peace, who fights for a meal of bread, who dies at a call of yes or no..."
>
> (Primo Levi; Se questo è un uomo, trans. 'If this is a man')

Primo Levi (1919-1987) was an Italian partisan, chemist and poet. He was of Jewish origin. He was captured in 1943 by Nazi supporters and deported to Auschwitz. 'If this is a Man' was the work he wrote about his experience in Auschwitz. Levi died in 1987 from injuries sustained in a fall from a third story apartment landing. His death was officially reported as suicide, though some of his supporters dispute this. He was also famous for his work as a chemist. His work 'The Periodic Table' (1975) was named by the Royal Institution of Great Britain as the best science book ever written. Yet he is most remembered for his work trying to inform the world of the cruelty of the camps. Levi was friendly with the philosopher Norberto Bobbio and Cesare Pavese who would become one of Italy's best known novelists.

Levi was among 650 Italian Jews who were deported to Auschwitz together. Levi was one of twenty who left the camps alive. In his 1982 novel (Se non ora, quando? trans. If not now, when?) Levi asks:

> "Eternal one, may you be held holy, why did you stay hidden behind the grey clouds instead of helping your people? You chose us from all the nations of the earth; why us? Why do the wicked prosper, are the defenceless unanswered, why hunger, the common graves, why power and why the flame throwers of the SS who fire into the hiding places of the terrified children?
>
> (Primo Levi, Se non ora, quando?" (Torino, 1982) p. 59)

In the many wars which afflict our world the terrified faces of the innocent who suffer (especially children) haunt the world. Levi was haunted by the plight of those who suffer and carried this pain with him all his life. His hope was that in recounting his agony, people would listen. Sadly this has not been the case and the agony continues. Many prefer to look the other way ("distraction from distraction" in the words of T.S. Eliot). Others rebel and say with Levi: 'where are you?'

From the Waste Land

Thomas Stearns Eliot (1888-1965), better known by his pen-name T.S. Eliot, was an American-born essayist, publisher, playwright, literary and social critic and one of the twentieth century's major poets. He settled in England in 1914, age 25, becoming a British citizen in 1927. He was awarded the Nobel Prize in Literature in 1948 for his "contribution to poetry". In the Four Quartets, one of his most famous poems, Eliot reminds us that humankind cannot bear very much reality. We often long to escape the hard questions and allow ourselves to be distracted. One author put this in an ironic title to his book "Amusing Ourselves to Death" (Neil Postman, London, 1985).

In October 1922 Eliot published 'The Waste Land'. It was written during a time of upheaval in Eliot's life. His marriage was failing and both he and his wife Vivienne were suffering from nervous disorders. The poem is often read as the disillusionment of the post-war generation. The poem comprises of the 'Burial of the Dead', 'A Game of Chess', 'The Fire Sermon', 'Death by Water', and 'What the Thunder Said'. The very beginning of the poem catches the bleakness of the Waste Land.

> "April is the cruelest month, breeding
> Lilacs out of the dead land, mixing
> Memory and desire, stirring
> Dull roots with spring rain."

The cruelty of the grave and loss are found in these words. The lilacs and the dead earth symbolise the grave. These are caught in the cruel April rain. This mood runs through the rest of the poem.

Compare this with the mood of the Four Quartets. This was written later and Eliot had come to find peace with God. He became an Anglo-Catholic in 1927. The 'Four Quartets' is a set of four poems written by Eliot over a six year period. The first poem 'Burnt Norton' was written in 1936, the others, 'East Coker', 'The Dry Salvages', and 'Little Gidding' were written during World War II. The poems were published together in 1943.

The concept of 'Burnt Norton' is time and the concept that time and only the present moment in time is what matters:

> "Time present and time past
> Are both perhaps present in time future,
> And time future contained in time past.
> If all time is eternally present
> All time is unredeemable...."

This is taken by some to refer to the eucharist. It is an event in time past (Jesus' death and resurrection) which is made present in the eucharist (time present) and redeems us and gives us confidence in the future. All time is not eternally present – therefore all time can be redeemed. In East Coker he refers to the "wounded surgeon". We learn this is Jesus when Eliot says "Again, in spite of that, we call this Friday good."

The Dry Salvages refers to a set of rocks Eliot would have seen in the sea near his New England home. He prays

> "Lady, whose shrine stands on the promontory,
> Pray for all those who are in ships, those
> Whose business has to do with fish..."

He asks Our Lady to protect all at sea, fishermen, those in the business world and those in need. He speaks later of the intersection of the 'timeless with time', the interceding of the infinite in the incarnation where God's word became flesh.

> "Here the impossible union
> Of spheres of existence is actual."

'Little Gidding' was a community of married people where life centered on the eucharist and the office. it was made up of families. In it Eliot says

> "The only hope, or else despair
> Lies in the choice of pyre or pyre –
> To be redeemed from fire by fire.
> Who then devised the torment? Love.
> Love is the unfamiliar Name
> Behind the hands that wove
> The intolerable shirt of flame
> Which human power cannot remove.
> We only live, only suspire
> Consumed by either fire or fire."

The 'fire' is desire, our desire for love. If we feel the fire of the lack of love then the fire of love, the Holy Spirit, is the fire by which we are redeemed. Hell is not to love and this burns, but the fire of love dissipates that fire. It is our choice which 'fire' we allow in. In the end he quotes Dame Julian of Norwich

> "All manner of things shall be well
> When the tongues of flame are in-folded
> Into the crowned knot of fire
> And the fire and the rose are one."

Again he refers to the Holy Spirit and the crown of thorns. There we experience love and in the fire of love all things will be well.

> "We shall not cease from exploration
> And the end of all our exploring
> Will be to arrive where we started."

There is a light that never goes out

Eliot's journey shows us that even in the deepest darkness the soul still finds light and new life is possible. Music and poetry and art often have healing effects on the soul. They enable us to express our feelings. John Keats spoke of "negative capability". By this he meant we learn to live with ambiguity and live with mystery. In many ways this goes against our age, because we want reality nailed down and defined, but this never happens. Music breaks these bonds and in ways we cannot define it moves us. In 2004 BBC Radio 4 looked at some of the songs that move us to cry, to shout out and to feel better.

One of the songs chosen was Leonard Cohen's 'Hallelujah' (1984). Cohen wrote the song and it appeared on the album 'Various Positions'. It found fame in cover versions by John Cale and later Jeff Buckley. Jeff Buckley describes how the song led him from loneliness to love. The song is about King David and his forbidden love for Bathsheba. The name 'Hallelujah' means praise Yahweh and is used in the psalms. Another song on the list was a song by The Smiths called 'There is a light that Never goes out' (1984) written by lead singer Morrissey and guitarist Johnny Marr. The Smiths catch a mood of sadness yet even here in the darkness a light shines. We cannot define how these songs work, yet they do. They often embrace the whole confusion of what life and love are. They also show us how strong the human spirit is in spite of all. God's Spirit is ever at work drawing new life from that which seems dead.

This helps us to appreciate the resurrection of Jesus. There is no account of the actual rising from the dead and our attempts to describe it are weak. We find ourselves before mystery. The resurrection is not, as many think, the resuscitation of a corpse. It is a new life. The old is left behind and Jesus now lives forever in a new, glorified form. The incident in St. Luke's Gospel of the two disciples on the road to Emmaus can teach us a lot:

> "Now on that same day two of them were going to a village called Emmaus, about seven miles from Jerusalem, and talking with each other about all these things that had happened. While they were talking and discussing, Jesus himself came near and went with them, but their eyes were kept from recognizing him. And he said to them, "What are you discussing with each other while you walk along?" They stood still, looking sad. Then one of them, whose name was Cleopas, answered him, "Are you the only stranger in Jerusalem who does not know the things that have taken place there in these days?" He asked them, "What things?" They replied, "The things about Jesus of Nazareth, who was a

prophet mighty in deed and word before God and all the people, and how our chief priests and leaders handed him over to be condemned to death and crucified him. But we had hoped that he was the one to redeem Israel. Yes, and besides all this, it is now the third day since these things took place. Moreover, some women of our group astounded us. They were at the tomb early this morning, and when they did not find his body there, they came back and told us that they had indeed seen a vision of angels who said that he was alive. Some of those who were with us went to the tomb and found it just as the women had said; but they did not see him." Then he said to them, "Oh, how foolish you are, and how slow of heart to believe all that the prophets have declared! Was it not necessary that the Messiah should suffer these things and then enter into his glory?" Then beginning with Moses and all the prophets, he interpreted to them the things about himself in all the scriptures. As they came near the village to which they were going, he walked ahead as if he were going on. But they urged him strongly, saying, "Stay with us, because it is almost evening and the day is now nearly over." So he went in to stay with them. When he was at the table with them, he took bread, blessed and broke it, and gave it to them. Then their eyes were opened, and they recognized him; and he vanished from their sight. They said to each other, "Were not our hearts burning within us while he was talking to us on the road, while he was opening the scriptures to us?" That same hour they got up and returned to Jerusalem; and they found the eleven and their companions gathered together. They were saying, "The Lord has risen indeed, and he has appeared to Simon!" Then they told what had happened on the road, and how he had been made known to them in the breaking of the bread.

(Lk 24:13-35)

Luke's account of Jesus' ministry before his death emphasises very much Jesus' going to Jerusalem. Here we have two disciples leave Jerusalem after Jesus' death. This symbolises losing hope and abandoning Jerusalem. Then Jesus comes and walks with them. He reminds them of his prophecy about being handed over (Lk 9:22; 13:32f, 18:31-33). The men describe how some women from their group claim to have seen Jesus risen, but they do not seem to believe the women. Jesus begins to speak then about Moses and all that was written. Jesus makes as if to go on, but they beg him to stay with them. They recognised him in the breaking of bread. Their hearts were set on fire by Jesus but Jesus disappeared. They realised they had encountered Jesus, risen and new and they returned to Jerusalem, the centre of Jesus' mission. They were renewed in Spirit. Their experience shows us the mystery of Jesus' new life after death but also the reality of his healing presence. They experienced the resurrection as the rebirth of hope. In Ezekiel (Ez 11:22-26) the prophet has a vision of God's glory, his presence, his shekinah, leave the temple. This was a harrowing vision for the Jewish people. Even though Herod rebuilt the Temple God's shekinah was not believed to have returned. This helps us understand the radicality of Paul's statement: "Did you not know that your bodies are temples of the Holy Spirit, who is in you, whom you have received from God." (1 Cor 6:19). The glory that lived in the temple is now in us. We are the temple of God. In the Gospel of John Jesus tells the disciples he will not leave them orphans:

> 'If you love me you will keep my commandments.
> I shall ask the Father,
> and he will give you another Paraclete
> to be with you for ever,
> the Spirit of truth
> whom the world can never accept
> since it neither sees nor knows him;
> but you know him,
> because he is with you, he is in you.
> I shall not leave you orphans;
> I shall come to you.
> In a short time the world will no longer see me;
> but you will see that I live
> and you also will live.
> On that day
> you will know that I am in my Father
> and you in me and I in you.
> Whoever holds to my commandments and keeps them
> is the one who loves me;
> and whoever loves me will be loved by my Father,
> and I shall love him and reveal myself to him.'

Judas – not Judas Iscariot – said to him, 'Lord, what has happened, that you intend to show yourself to us and not to the world?' Jesus replied:

> Anyone who loves me will keep my word,
> and my Father will love him,
> and we shall come to him
> and make a home in him.
>
> (Jn 14:15-23)

Jesus' command is that we love one another as he has loved us (Jn 13:33f). God lives in our innermost being by the power of the Holy Spirit. This complements the saying of Paul. This shows the love God has for us and the love we should have for ourselves and others. In another song by Leonard Cohen, Anthem (1992) he tells us

> "There is a crack in everything
> That's how the light gets in."

In the brokenness of our lives and loves light breaks in and we find strength. "Hallelujah".

Losing and Finding:

Ps 73 is described as a psalm of Asaph. Asaph was one of the singers appointed by David (1 Chron 6:39) and is credited with performing at the dedication of Solomon's temple in 2 Chronicles 5:12. Jacquet says that Ps 73 goes further than Job in his battle to understand God's ways. It goes further than Qoheleth (Ecclesiastes) who leaves us feeling a void in our hearts. The psalmist finds in his heart the love of God and this gives meaning to his existence (Jacquet, II, p. 436). In God we experience the probability of joy and life eternal in love. God is the one who leads me (Ps 73:23-24). The Islamic mystic Al-Hallaj (+922) says: "Your place in my heart is my complete heart".

Yet before the psalmist reaches the place of peace he is distracted and confused by the darkness he experiences. He is tempted to give up and live an empty life – a life empty of love.

Psalm *Of Asaph*

Indeed God is good to Israel,
the Lord to those who are pure of heart.

My feet were on the point of stumbling,
a little more and I had slipped,
envying the arrogant as I did,
and seeing the prosperity of the wicked.

For them no such thing as pain,
untroubled, their comfortable portliness;
exempt from the cares which are the human lot,
they have no part in Adam's afflictions.

So pride is a necklace to them,
violence the garment they wear.
From their fat oozes out malice,
their hearts drip with cunning.

Cynically they advocate evil,
loftily they advocate force.
Their mouth claims heaven for themselves,
and their tongue is never still on earth.

That is why my people turn to them,
and enjoy the waters of plenty,
saying, 'How can God know?
What knowledge can the Most High have?'
That is what the wicked are like,
piling up wealth without any worries.

Was it useless, then, to have kept my own heart clean,
to have washed my hands in innocence?

When I was under a hail of blows all day long,
and punished every morning,
had I said, 'I shall talk like them,'
I should have betrayed your children's race.

So I set myself to understand this:
how difficult I found it!
Until I went into the sanctuaries of the gods
and understood what was destined to become of them.
You place them on a slippery slope
and drive them down into chaos.

How sudden their hideous destruction!
They are swept away, annihilated by terror!
Like a dream upon waking, Lord,
when you awake, you dismiss their image.

My heart grew embittered,
my affections dried up,
I was stupid and uncomprehending,
a clumsy animal in your presence.

(Ps 73:1-22)

The psalm begins positively speaking of how good Israel's God is. He refers to the pure in heart. The spirituality of the psalm is interior (see Ps 7:10; 17:3; 26:3) and from this arises praise in the liturgy (see Ps 106:1; 118:1,22; 135:1; 136:1 etc.). In the Gospel of Matthew we read: "Blessed are the pure in heart, they shall see God" (Matt 5:8).

Yet this faith has been called into question. One of the Old Testament teachings was about the dogma of retribution (see Ps 37:1; 49:6-7; Jer 12:1-2; Pro 3:31; 23:17) yet he does not see this. He has lost the peace, the shalom, of being with God. He looks at the unjust and how week they do and he is tempted to jealousy. Looking at how well the wicked seem they seem to be the ones who have peace. They seem immune from human fragility (see Job 1:11; 2:5; 4:3; 5:19). They flaunt their arrogant pride (Ps 10:2; 36:12). Yet this leads their hearts to harden, neither loving nor receiving love. The empty have a group to shore them up but ultimately they must face their own emptiness. In Isaiah we read: "Woe to those who burrow down, to conceal their plans from Yahweh, who scheme in the dark, and say "Who can see us? Who knows who we are?" (Is 29:15). We can deceive ourselves but not ultimately forever. Atheism in the sense of denying God is a temptation. We are reminded of Levi's cry "Where are you?" There is a profound battle taking place in the heart of the psalmist.

Yet the complaint itself is a prayer. He is not ashamed to bring his fears and doubts into prayer and in the silence awaits God's response.

Often it is the just who suffer. The prophet Malachi says: "... it is useless to serve God, what is the good of keeping his commandments or walking mournfully before Yahweh Sabaoth. In fact we now call the proud the happy ones; the evil doers the ones who prosper; they put God to the test, yet they come to no harm" (Mal 3:14f). Those who pray and worship are often those who suffer. For the psalmist of Ps 73 his present experience is full of bitterness (73:13-16). He has sought the mystery of life but he is like Qoholeth: "I have scrutinised God's whole creation, you cannot get to the bottom of everything taking place under the sun; you may wear yourself out in the search, but you will never find it. Not even a sage can get to the bottom of it..." (Ecclesiastes 8:17).

In verses 17-22 the psalmist has literally a change of heart. In the midst of his fear and doubt he meets God. "[The wicked] do not know the hidden things of God, they do not hope for the reward of holiness, they do not believe in a reward for blameless souls" (Wis 2:22). Jesus praises God for revealing his mysteries to the small ones: "I bless you, Father, Lord of heaven and earth, for hiding these things from the learned and clever and revealing them to little children" (Mtt 11:25). To the little ones has been revealed the mysteries of the kingdom of God (Mtt 13:11). The heart is the centre of one's being. The heart is the sanctuary where God and human beings meet in peace. We are often troubled but Jesus tells us: "Come to me, all you who labour and are overburdened and I will give you rest. Shoulder my yoke and learn from me for I am gentle and humble in heart, and you will find rest for your souls. Yes, my yoke is easy and my burden light" (Mtt 11:28f). In the darkness we meet this Jesus who is risen and whose presence is given to us in the Holy Spirit. The love of God poured into our hearts by the Holy Spirit given us heals us and helps us re-focus. God's love is in our hearts and our home is with him. When the psalmist drifts from this vision he becomes, as he says, almost a beast.

In George Bernanos' novel 'The Diary of a Country Priest' he tells us 'Hell is not to love anymore'. The priest experiences the darkness of which St. Thérèse spoke, the darkness of the suffering servant (Isa 52:13-53:12) and the suffering of Jesus. In the novel the Countess is one who is in hell. She is lost in grief over her daughter's death and wants to curse God. The timid priest confronts her and tells her that God in Jesus has suffered hell but still loves. She is released from her pain. Even those in this hell are sought by God. The novel finishes with the words of St. Thérèse: "All is grace". The psalm ends celebrating the faith of the just one in God, the pure of heart:

> "Even so, I stayed in your presence,
> you grasped me by the right hand;
> you will guide me with advice,
> and will draw me in the wake of your glory.
>
> Who else is there for me in heaven?
> And, with you, I lack nothing on earth.
> My heart and my flesh are pining away:
> my heart's rock, my portion, God for ever!
>
> Truly, those who abandon you will perish;
> you destroy those who adulterously desert you,
> whereas my happiness is to be near God.
> I have made the Lord Yahweh my refuge,
> to tell of all your works. (Ps 73:23-28)

His peace in God has released him from his rebellion and his assumptions that all is well with the unjust. He is now eternally present to God who is present to him. He has discovered the indwelling God at the centre of his being. Isaiah says of God: "I Yahweh will take you by the hand" (Isa 42:6)

Psalm 37 speaks as follows: "When he trips [the just one] he is not thrown sprawling, since Yahweh supports him by the hand (Ps 37:24). The psalmist has met this God. Eternal life is to know this God and Jesus Christ whom he sent (Jn 17:3). St. Irenaeus said that the glory of God is a human being fully alive. When the psalmist speaks of God's glory, his 'kabod', it is in this sense that he means it. In God's love the psalmist has become an authentic human being. It is in God's love we dwell. Those who do not love leave this place, but even then God seeks their healing and salvation. All is grace, as St. Thérèse reminds us. We are all loved infinitely by God. This is the heart of the message of Jesus and the love of God is poured into our hearts by the 'Holy Spirit given us' (Rom 5:5).

> Tout est grâce
> 'All is grace'

Chapter 7

Riders on the Storm

> "Over a half-century ago, when I was still a child, I recall hearing a number of old people offer the following explanation for the great disasters that had befallen Russia: 'Men have forgotten God: that's why all this has happened.' Since then I have spent well-nigh 50 years working on the history of our revolution; in the process I have read hundreds of books, collated hundreds of personal testimonies … But if I were asked today to formulate as concisely as possible the main cause of the ruinous revolution that swallowed up some 60 million of our people, I could not put it more accurately than to repeat: 'Men have forgotten God: that's why all this has happened.'"
>
> (see E.E. Ericsson, Solzhenitsyn – Voice from the Gulag, Eternity (October 1985) pp. 23-24)

Alexander Solzhenitsyn (1918-2008) was a Russian writer who raised global awareness of the Gulag forced labour system in his work. He was awarded the Nobel prize for literature in 1970 "for the ethical force with which he has pursued the indispensable traditions of Russian literature" (Nobel Laudatum, 17th October 2008). He was expelled from the Soviet Union in 1974, but returned to Russia in 1994 after the dissolution of the Soviet Union. During his life he was a political prisoner and exile under Stalin because of remarks he had made about Stalin in private letters.

Matryona's Home is a short story written by Solzhenitsyn in 1959. The story and the characters are not invented but come from real life. Ignatich, the narrator, closely parallels Solzhenitsyn as an ex-prisoner who is now released but is exiled is Kazakhstan and takes lodgings with Matryona in the village of Miltsevo.

Matryona is a victim of the petty and tawdry villagers who use Matryona. Her life has been a life full of suffering but this has not beaten her down. She consistently exhibits moral nobility as she overcomes adversity, lives in harmony with nature. She helps those in need and she harms no-one. She does not speak of religion but Ignatich knows she prays silently when she thinks he is asleep. In this atmosphere Ignatich comes to himself and finds healing and peace.

Matryona is forced by a relative to give a small annex of her home to a relative who wants the wood. A group of farmers who are drunk decide to move the wood at night. Matryona tries to help but is killed in an accident. It was the end of the story which moved me:

> "We all lived beside her, and never understood that she was
> the righteous one without whom, according to the proverb,
> no village can stand.
> Nor any city.
> Nor our whole world."

There is a tradition that goes back to Genesis 18 that there are a number of righteous, good people who sustain the world. I have found it in Judaism, Christianity and Islam. Genesis 18 is where Abraham bargained with God about the just one praying for the people. Matryona was one such for Solzhenitsyn. Her gentle care helped me recover from cancer and her tenderness soothed his soul. Her prayer led him to faith, to find again the faith of his youth. There are people who have not forgotten God and through them God reaches others.

Dark is the World to me

We live in a world of confusion. We live "east of Eden". We say we admire courage, integrity and self-sacrifice for others. Yet in practice these are the very things that in this land east of Eden go unrewarded. John Steinbeck puts it as follows:

"There is a strange duality in the human which makes for an ethical paradox. We have definitions of good qualities and of bad; not changing things, but generally considered good and bad throughout the ages and throughout the species. Of the good, we think always of wisdom, tolerance, kindliness, generosity, humility; and the qualities of cruelty, greed, self-interest, graspingness, and rapacity are universally considered undesirable. And yet in our structure of society, the so-called and considered good qualities are invariable concomitants of failure, while the bad ones are the cornerstones of success. A man – a viewing-point man – while he will love the abstract good qualities and detest the abstract bad, will nevertheless envy and admire the person who through possessing the abstract bad qualities has succeeded economically and socially, and will hold in contempt that person whose good qualities have caused failure. When such a viewing-point man thinks of Jesus or St. Augustine or Socrates he regards them with love because they are the symbols of the good he admires, and he hates the symbols of the bad. But actually he would rather be successful than good. In an animal other than man we would replace the term "good" with "weak survival quotient" and the term "bad" with "strong survival quotient." Thus, man in his thinking or reverie status admires the progression towards extinction, but in the unthinking stimulus which really activates him he tends toward survival. Perhaps no other animal is so torn between alternatives. **Man might be described fairly adequately, if simply, as a two-legged paradox. He has never become accustomed to the tragic miracle of consciousness. Perhaps, as has been suggested, his species is not set, has not jelled, but is still in a state of becoming, bound by his physical memories to a past of struggle and survival, limited in his futures by the uneasiness of thought and consciousness."**

(John Steinbeck, The Log from the Sea of Cortez (New York: 1951) cited in TD2, p. 336f).

This describes the fundamental fault that we find in the centre of our being. In Thucydides (460-400 BC), the ancient Greek historian, he recounts the following dialogue between the Athenians and the Melians (v, 85-112), the standpoint of the strongest party is opposed to that of fairness and sincerity.

> "Do not imagine that we are ignorant that, among men, there can only be justice where powers are equal; **the powerful man does what suits him, and the weak man must put up with it... In our view the right of the stronger applies to the whole world and to the divinity in which we believe, and this accords with man's experience...** Nor should you clutch at the notion of honor, which has so often brought imperilled men to ruin; many a one has been incited, by the seductive sound of the word "honour" freely to plunge forever to his own destruction..."

After the battle the men of Melos were slaughtered.

Abraham Joshua Heschel (1907-1973) was a Polish-born American rabbi. In October 1938 he emigrated first to London before heading to the United States. Heschel's sister was killed in a German bombing raid. His mother was murdered by the Nazis, and his two sisters, Gittel and Dvora, died in the concentration camps. He never returned to Poland: "If I should go to Germany or Poland, every stone, every tree would remind me of contempt, hatred, murder of children,..."

Heschel arrived in New York in March 1940. He served on the faculty of the Hebrew Union College (HUC), the main seminary of Reform Judaism. In 1946 he took up a position at the Jewish Theological Seminary of America (JTS) in New York. He married Sylvia Strauss, a concert pianist, in 1946. Their daughter Susannah became a scholar in her own right. Heschel in his writings sought to bring human beings into the presence of God and see their dignity therein. He was also an important voice for the document of Vatican II on Christian-Jewish dialogue (Nostra Aetate).

One of the central questions in his writings was: what does it mean to be human? He says we have abandoned holiness for convenience, loyalty for success, love for power, wisdom for information, tradition for fashion (Man's Quest for God, p. 150). In our age of internet, Facebook, Twitter, we live out Heschel's prophecy – never so much information, never so little communication. We live in an age which legislates against homicide, yet we wage war with ferocity and slaughter whole peoples. Western society tends to look on people for their utility. This is why it is hard to understand Heschel when he speaks of time as the border of eternity, or when he urges us to live this single moment as if all our existence depended on it. Human life is holy, a holiness that comes as God's gift. Yet human life is discarded with the greatest of ease. While disease and starvation afflict two thirds of the human race we build luxury hotels, gambling casinos. The Baal Shem Tov warns us "Replete is the world with spiritual radiance, replete with sublime and marvelous secrets. But a small hand held up against the eye hides it all." Insensitivity is increasing exponentially and true humanity is broken causing many to take their lives. In the face of this Heschel says "Human life is he who is concerned with other selves." (Man is not alone, p. 138). There is in our hearts a great uneasiness at the insensitivity of the world.

Are we alone in this maze of self, alone in the wilderness of time, alone in the silent universe, of which we are a part and yet in which we so often feel like strangers? Is there no-one to collect the tears, understand the agony of the innocent, the poor, the sorrowing? Is there no Presence worth living for, no Presence worth dying for, no way of being compatible with this Presence? The Presence he refers to is that of God. Heschel says: "Personal needs come and go, but one anxiety remains: Am I needed? Every human being has been moved by that anxiety to a greater or lesser degree." (Man is not Alone, p. 193). The quest for meaning is to understand oneself as well as the whole of humanity in terms larger than the self. To be human is to become involved, to act, to love, to wonder, to respond. We sense a Presence greater than us calling us. Biblical thought seeks to relate humanity to a transcendence called the living God. The meaning of our existence depends on whether or not we respond to God who is in search of us.

> "Over and above personal problems, there is an objective challenge to overcome inequity, injustice, helplessness, suffering, carelessness, oppression. Over and above the din of desires, there is a calling, a demanding, a waiting, an expectation. There is a question that follows me wherever I turn. What is expected of me? What is demanded of me?... Over and above all things is a sublime expectation, a waiting for. With every child born a new expectation enters the world."
>
> (Insecurity of Freedom, p. 49)

The process of creation is not complete. God's dream is not yet attained. There is a cry for justice that only we can answer. There is a need for gentleness, for compassion, for understanding that only we can satisfy. We are God's representatives. We need a sense of beauty and joy. In this regard Heschel cites the words of Wiliam Wordsworth:

> "To me the meanest flower that blows can give
> Thoughts that do often lie too deep for tears."

Blake's words too help us:

> "To see the world in a grain of sand,
> And a Heaven in a wild flower
> Hold infinity in the palm of your hand
> And eternity in an hour."

We have cast aside wonder. When we recover wonder we can stand in the Presence, allowing ourselves to commune, to receive a ray of God's glory and to reflect it. (Man is not Alone, p. 88-91, 271f). Hardness and callousness to the mystery around us, boredom at the gifts of life, apathy to the people who touch our lives are obstacles to the life of faith. Faith is rooted in the passionate care for the marvel that is everywhere, a care that extends to all realms of life. Faith seeks to see the transcendent within the world. This is what St. Francis did when he saw God in all things.

The will to power and domination form part of our world, but we are slowly realising that these are destroying us. There is a passion for arrogance and cruelty that only the awe and fear of God can soothe, there is a suffocating greed in humanity that only holiness can suffuse, that liberty without righteousness and compassion is terrifying, that humanity without God is meaningless. The mystery of God's omnipotence hovers over the whole of revelation. From God came the mystery of a divine utterance, and a word, a sound which reached the ear of the prophet. Just as the Spirit of his creative power brought the world into being, so too the Spirit of his revealing power brought the Bible into being (God in Search of Man, 172-181). Our human destiny is to become a partner with God in making God's Presence real in mercy, gentleness, care and compassion.

Heschel speaks of God's pathos in his 1962 work "The Prophets". The prophet is one who hears God's voice and he feels God's heart (God in Search of Man, p. 21). Heschel explains God's pathos as follows:

> "To the prophet... God does not reveal himself in an abstract absoluteness, but in a personal and intimate relation to the world. He does not simply command and expect obedience; He is also moved and affected by what happens in the world, and reacts accordingly... Quite obviously in the biblical view, man's deeds may move Him, affect Him, grieve Him or, on the other hand, gladden and please Him. This notion that God can be intimately affected, that He possesses not merely intelligence and will, but also pathos, basically defines the prophetic consciousness of God."
>
> (The Prophets, p. 222ff)

Heschel tells us "God does not stand outside the range of human suffering and sorrow. He is personally involved in, even stirred by, the conduct and fate of men" (Prophets, p. 224). History is often the record of human misery and God is involved in this suffering. God's participation in human history finds its deepest expression in the fact that God can actually suffer (Prophets, p. 259). The anguish of God echoes throughout the Bible. By way of example Heschel comments on

Isaiah 42:14 – "From long ago I have been silent, I have kept quiet, held myself in check, groaning like a woman in labour, panting and gasping for air." This shows the immensity of God's suffering. God is involved in all human suffering. As Isaiah says: "In all their afflictions He was afflicted" (Isa 63:9) (see Prophets, p. 151). God is full of compassion. He is our companion and a fellow sufferer who understands.

Heschel says "The pagan gods heed selfish needs, while the God of Israel is only in need of man's integrity. The need of Moloch was the death of men, the need of the Lord is the life of men" (Man is not Alone, p. 245). The divine pathos which the prophets tried to express in many ways was not a name for his essence but rather for the mode of his reaction to Israel's conduct which would change if Israel modified its ways (Man is not Alone, p. 245). This does not mean that the divine essence is changeable but God who is in relation with his creation can be moved in his heart, his innermost being. He suffers because he cares – his nature is love.

When the prophet hears God's voice and feels God's heart we hear them rage against the mistreatment of the widow, against manipulation of the worker, against callousness towards the poor – in reality an attempt to express how much God suffers in all these events. We look upon acts of cheating in business, or lying, as something slight that we expect and overlook: to the prophets, feeling with the heart of God, such events are a disaster. We live in a world where there is an abysmal indifference to evil.

What might appear to us as exaggeration in the prophet is in reality a glimpse of God's concern and sharing in the plight of humanity. Humankind writhes in agony. Yet the prophet becomes the voice that speaks for the poor, to the agony of creation profaned by the powerful and wealthy. God has thrust a burden upon the soul of the prophet, the burden of his concern, of his vision, and the prophet is bowed down by the fierce greed that is around us. Behind the condemnation of the prophet lies the rage of God (Prophets, p. 4f).

This God demands justice for his people because of his great love. His love for justice is rooted in his compassion for humanity. Injustice is condemned, not because a law has been broken, but because a human being is being harmed. The preoccupation of the prophets with justice and their passionate condemnation of injustice grows out of their sympathy with the divine pathos. He participates in the very life of God.

For Heschel, without a God who cares, our universe becomes an inferno. No human ear can catch the cry of agony of so many suffering people. The callousness and hardness of the world as many of us find is a profound failure. One could not bear or endure so much misery, so much callousness, were it not for the certainty in faith that God listens to our cry. The basic insight of biblical faith, the mystery and grandeur of the infinite concern of God for his people, is essential to our sanity and our survival. God is immediately and personally concerned. We are not alone (Prophets, p. 219f). Our life is a life shared with God. Humanity is charged with God's mission, we are chosen as God's partner in history. Justice, mercy and compassion are not just human conventions or values. They are a transcendent demand, reflecting the divine concern. These events involve God. To be merciful, to love, to be just, makes us partners with God (see Prophets p. 198-201). Our task is to bring God into our world and our lives.

The Bible is a never-ending expression of God's concern for humanity. It is not so much a book to be read as a drama in which we are called to participate. Our participation is our response to God's call. God confronts all of us in the words of the prophets. When he addressed the prophets, he addressed each one of us. This enables us to acknowledge "Here is the presence of God" (God in Search of Man, p. 253-255).

A New Person in Christ

Soren Kierkegaard (1813-1855) spoke of the infinite distance that separates our limited minds from the vastness of God. Yet God has reached down to us in the form of his word to the prophets and his Word made flesh. He wrote in his journals:

> "The Hegelian babble about the real being the true is therefore the same kind of confusion as when people assume that the words and actions of a poet's dramatic characters are the poet's own. We must, however, hold fast to the belief that when God – so to speak – decides to write a play, he does not do it simply in order to pass the time, as the pagans thought. No, no: indeed, the utterly serious point here is that loving and being loved is God's passion. It is almost – infinite love! – as if he is bound to this passion, almost as if it were a weakness on his part; whereas in fact it is his strength, his almighty love: and in that respect his love is subject to no alteration of any kind.
> There is a staggering perversity in all the human categories that are applied to the God-man; for if we could speak in a completely human way about Christ we would have to say that the words "My God, my God, why have you forsaken me?" show a want of patient and a want of truth. Only if God says it, can it be true, i.e., even if the God-man says it. And since it is true, it is also truly the climax of pain.
> The relationship to God is evidently such a tremendous weight of blessedness that, once I have laid hold of it, it is absolute in the most absolute sense; by contrast, the worldly notion that my enemies are to be excluded from it would actually diminish this blessedness."
>
> The Journals of Soren Kierkegaard

God's words are like love letters, he said. Barth (who was influenced by Kierkegaard) said that the Bible was the word of God in the words of men.

Jesus died, rose from the dead by the power of the Holy Spirit and lives in eternity in loving union with the Father in the love of the Spirit. He is ever active calling us to new life, to be a new creation. We see this in the apostle Paul. In the Acts of the Apostles we read how Jesus met Paul.

> Meanwhile Saul was still breathing threats to slaughter the Lord's disciples. He went to the high priest and asked for

letters addressed to the synagogues in Damascus, that would authorise him to arrest and take to Jerusalem any followers of the Way, men or women, that he might find.
It happened that while he was travelling to Damascus and approaching the city, suddenly a light from heaven shone all round him. He fell to the ground, and then he heard a voice saying, 'Saul, Saul, why are you persecuting me?' 'Who are you, Lord?' he asked, and the answer came, 'I am Jesus, whom you are persecuting. Get up and go into the city, and you will be told what you are to do.' The men travelling with Saul stood there speechless, for though they heard the voice they could see no one. Saul got up from the ground, but when he opened his eyes he could see nothing at all, and they had to lead him into Damascus by the hand. For three days he was without his sight and took neither food nor drink.
There was a disciple in Damascus called Ananias, and he had a vision in which the Lord said to him, 'Ananias!' When he replied, 'Here I am, Lord,' the Lord said, 'Get up and go to Straight Street and ask at the house of Judas for someone called Saul, who comes from Tarsus. At this moment he is praying, and has seen a man called Ananias coming in and laying hands on him to give him back his sight.'
But in response, Ananias said, 'Lord, I have heard from many people about this man and all the harm he has been doing to your holy people in Jerusalem. He has come here with a warrant from the chief priests to arrest everybody who invokes your name.' The Lord replied, 'Go, for this man is my chosen instrument to bring my name before gentiles and kings and before the people of Israel; I myself will show him how much he must suffer for my name.' Then Ananias went. He entered the house, and laid his hands on Saul and said, 'Brother Saul, I have been sent by the Lord Jesus, who appeared to you on your way here, so that you may recover your sight and be filled with the Holy Spirit.' It was as though scales fell away from his eyes and

immediately he was able to see again. So he got up and was baptised, and after taking some food he regained his strength.

(Acts 9:1-18)

The conversion of Paul or his call is given here. There are two other accounts of his call – one in 22:14-16 and in 26:15-18. In the account in chapter 9 Saul was still threatening the early church. Then he was blinded by a light. He heard a voice asking why was he persecuting him? This was Jesus who by the power of the Spirit appeared to Paul. The dreaded persecutor was now immobilsed and was a remorseful penitent. Ananias is afraid when he hears of Paul, but he trusts and by the power of the Holy Spirit heals Paul. N.T. Wright shows how this encounter with the risen Jesus transformed him and that he rethought his Jewish heritage in the light of his experience of encounter with the one who was dead, but is now alive and whose presence is mediated by the Spirit.[1] Paul says in the first letter to the Corinthians:

> "there is only one God, the Father from whom all things come and for whom we exist, and one Lord, Jesus Christ, through whom all things come and through whom we exist"
>
> (1 Cor 8:6)

N.T. Wright argues that Romans 6-8 as a whole constitutes (among other things) a re-telling of the Exodus story.[2] It starts on the journey in which the slaves are set free (chapter 6) up to the mountain where the torch is given but then Moses is confronted by the sin of the people, making idols in place of Yahweh (chapter 7). He sees parallels with the people grumbling and wanting to go back to the old ways: He speaks of the new way of the Spirit who makes us children of God.

> All who are guided by the Spirit of God are sons of God; for what you received was not the spirit of slavery to bring you back into fear; you received the Spirit of adoption, enabling

[1] N.T. Wright, Paul and the Faithfulness of God (London: 2013).

[2] N.T. Wright, Paul and the Faithfulness of God, Rec 1799 on Kindle.

> us to cry out, 'Abba, Father!' The Spirit himself joins with our spirit to bear witness that we are children of God. And if we are children, then we are heirs, heirs of God and joint-heirs with Christ, provided that we share his suffering, so as to share his glory.
>
> (Rom 8:14-17)

The events of Jesus and the Spirit have unveiled the one true God and who we are. He begins chapter 8 with the following lines (following Wright's translation):

> "So therefore there is no condemnation for those in the Messiah Jesus. Why not? Because the law of the Spirit of life in the Messiah released you from the law of sin and death."
>
> (Rom 8:1-2)

The law (torah) given by God to Moses showed the weakness of humanity so

> For God has done what the law (weak because of human sin) was incapable of doing. God sent his own son in the likeness of sinful flesh, and as a sin offering, he condemned sin. This was in order that the right and proper verdict of the law could be fulfilled in us, as we live not according to the flesh, but according to the Spirit."
>
> (Rom 8:3-4)

Jesus participates in the emptiness and negativity of life and overcomes death. He is the one who accepts us and loves us and by the sending of the Spirit makes us children of God.

Wright continues and tells us that there are parallels with the Book of Wisdom and what Paul is saying here (loc. 17 947f). The opening six chapters of the Book of Wisdom portray the wicked who kill the righteous, but they are confronted with the resurrected righteous themselves who are shown to be 'sons of God'. Wisdom is what the earth's rulers require and there is a testimony ascribed to Solomon that he gained wisdom through his prayers (Wisdom 7:1-22). Wisdom is a "spotless mirror of the working of God, an image of his goodness" (Wisdom 7:26). Then we listen to Solomon's prayer. The heart of the prayer is a request for wisdom so that Solomon might know God's will.

> With you is Wisdom, she who knows your works,
> she who was present when you made the world;
> she understands what is pleasing in your eyes
> and what agrees with your commandments.
> Despatch her from the holy heavens,
> send her forth from your throne of glory
> to help me and to toil with me
> and teach me what is pleasing to you;
> since she knows and understands everything
> she will guide me prudently in all my actions
> and will protect me with her glory.
> Then all I do will be acceptable,
> I shall govern your people justly
> and be worthy of my father's throne.
>
> What human being indeed can know the intentions of God?
> And who can comprehend the will of the Lord?
> For the reasoning of mortals is inadequate,
> our attitudes of mind unstable;
> for a perishable body presses down the soul,
> and this tent of clay weighs down the mind with its many cares.
> It is hard enough for us to work out what is on earth,
> laborious to know what lies within our reach;
> who, then, can discover what is in the heavens?
> And who could ever have known your will, had you not given Wisdom
> and sent your holy Spirit from above?
> Thus have the paths of those on earth been straightened
> and people have been taught what pleases you,
> and have been saved, by Wisdom.
>
> (Wisdom 9:9-17)

By receiving the Spirit we are incorporated into Christ. We begin a new life. Paul spoke of his new life, his transformation in Jesus. He said: "The life I am now living, subject to the libation of human nature I am living in faith, faith in the Son of God who loved me and gave himself for me." (Gal 2:20f). He is now in communion with Jesus. In Romans 5:5 he speaks of the love of God poured into our hearts by the Spirit who has been given to us. He speaks here of his experience and now he is in communion with Jesus and led by his Spirit. He says in the same passage from Galatians: "I have been crucified with Christ, and yet I am alive; yet it is no longer I but Christ living in me (Gal 2:20a). In Philippians he writes about coming to know Jesus the Christ and his love.

> ...as for religious fervour, I was a persecutor of the Church; as for the uprightness embodied in the Law, I was faultless. But what were once my assets I now through Christ Jesus count as losses. Yes, I will go further: because of the supreme advantage of knowing Christ Jesus my Lord, I count everything else as loss. For him I have accepted the loss of all other things, and look on them all as filth if only I can gain Christ and be given a place in him, with the uprightness I have gained not from the Law, but through faith in Christ, an uprightness from God, based on faith, that I may come to know him and the power of his resurrection, and partake of his sufferings by being moulded to the pattern of his death, striving towards the goal of resurrection from the dead. Not that I have secured it already, nor yet reached my goal, but I am still pursuing it in the attempt to take hold of the prize for which Christ Jesus took hold of me. Brothers, I do not reckon myself as having taken hold of it; I can only say that forgetting all that lies behind me, and straining forward to what lies in front, I am racing towards the finishing-point to win the prize of God's heavenly call in Christ Jesus. So this is the way in which all of us who are mature should be thinking, and if you are still thinking differently in any way, then God has yet to make this matter clear to you. Meanwhile, let us go forward from the point we have each attained.
>
> (Phil 3:6-16)

Paul uses the expression "in Christ" (en Christo) to signify his new life in union with the resurrected Jesus by the power of the Holy Spirit. The phrase "by the Spirit" (en pneumati) is virtually synonymous with the phrase in Christ in the writings of Paul. In 1 Cor 6:17 he says: "anyone who attaches himself to the Lord is one spirit with him". In the passage quoted from Philippians above Paul sees his life as a communion with the life, death and resurrection of Jesus. By giving himself to God through Jesus in the Spirit, Paul is renewed and becomes a new man (it is no longer I who live, but Christ in me). Through his life as an apostle he becomes the person God called him to be. This concept of 'person' is important for Von Balthasar. In his work on Theodrama he emphasizes the importance of 'role'. God has called us to be his partners and given us a role to play. Jesus is the primary actor in God's Theodrama (TD3, p. 15). In life Jesus' role is his 'mission' for God. He sees 'mission' as constituting the person. God has given Jesus a mission and 'in Jesus' we too have a mission in him. Balthasar unfolds the analogy based on the motivation of an individual, conscious subject who comes to know who they are through their interaction with others, and through the acceptance of commitments, goals and acts of love. The child is brought to life through the smile of the mother and grows in the love of others and self if cared for. Ultimately Von Balthasar argues the constitution of the conscious subject as a person, secure in their identity, can only be accomplished by interaction with God. His love is poured into our hearts:

> It is when God addresses a conscious subject, tells him who he is and what he means to the eternal God of truth and shows him the purpose of his existence – *that is, imparts a distinctive and divinely authorised mission* – that we can say of a conscious subject that he is a "person". This is what happened, archetypically, in the case of Jesus Christ, when he was given his eternal "definition" – "You are my beloved Son" (TD3, p. 207)

What makes the Son who he is from all eternity, is his reception from the Father of everything that he is. In his giving of himself to the Father in his earthly mission he is the one who is open, who receives and obeys and fulfills what the Father asked of him. His mission is to be the Son.

Human beings blossom as persons by being known and loved and have a purpose in life. We can see Jesus' full humanity is activated by living out his mission as the Son in response to the Father's love.

When we enter into communion with Jesus, like Paul, we discover who we are through our mission in life. In Paul's image of the body (1 Cor 12) we see each one of us has a part. Von Balthasar uses Paul's 'in Christ' to help us see who we are in God's eyes. By dying to self and giving ourselves to God, we become alive as new people, a new creation (2 Cor 5:17). Person is the new name by which God addresses me (Rev 2:17). It also implies I have been given a role in Christ to be "a pillar in the temple of my God" (Rev 3:12). All people are included in the "theo-drama in the person of Christ" (TD3, p. 203). Jesus' own mission is his acceptance of others which means that what he sees in his fellow man is primarily what this man is intended to be in the plan of the divine Father ... and what he, the Son is to achieve by taking upon himself this sinful hiatus. Jesus' I-Thous relationship with his fellow man is rooted in his I-Thou relationship in the Spirit with the Father (TD3, 179). We are included in this mission of bringing all people to peace with God – each having a role, a mission in Christ. Von Balthasar speaks of how an artist or a scholar is so possessed by his vocation that he is free and inspired to carry out his work in love (TD3, p. 225).

Our Hope

In a passage in Romans 8 Paul says:

> We are well aware that the whole creation, until this time, has been groaning in labour pains. And not only that: we too, who have the first-fruits of the Spirit, even we are groaning inside ourselves, waiting with eagerness for our bodies to be set free. In hope, we already have salvation; in hope, not visibly present, or we should not be hoping – nobody goes on hoping for something which is already visible. But having this hope for what we cannot yet see, we are able to wait for it with persevering confidence.

(Rom 8:22-26)

Paul here shows us our salvation is not just personal. God wills to save all people and the entire creation. Our lives in Christ my appear insignificant to us but we have not learned to see ourselves as God sees us. We are involved by God in making all things new.

The Book of Revelation complements Paul's teaching. In the first four chapters we hear the Spirit speak to the Churches in what appears to be just local letters. Yet chapters 4-19 show us that the churches are involved in the battle between God and evil and so are we. In chapter 19 the new Jerusalem the symbol of God's success is dressed in linen "made of the good deeds of the Saints" (Rev 19:8). God incorporates us into his work of healing the whole of creation. When God's victory to which we look forward is final then:

> Then I saw a new heaven and a new earth, the first heaven and the first earth had disappeared now, and there was no longer any sea. I saw the holy city, the new Jerusalem, coming down out of heaven from God, prepared as a bride dressed for her husband. Then I heard a loud voice call from the throne, 'Look, here God lives among human beings. He will make his home among them, they will be his people, and he will be their God, God-with-them. He will wipe away all tears from their eyes, there will be no more death, and no more mourning or sadness or pain. The world of the past has gone.'
>
> (Rev 21:1-4)

The new heaven and the new earth is a fulfillment of the prophet Isaiah 66:17-25. There is a radical discontinuity here – the old world is gone but from the old has grown a whole new creation. The world of chaos and violence has passed and a new order is established. A voice from the throne interprets the vision by showing the fulfillment of old promises (see Lev 26:11-12; Ez 37:27 and 2 Cor 6:16). Wiping away tears and bringing peace is the fulfillment of God's plan for our healing and salvation (see Isa 25:8 and Rev 7:17). Our happiness is God's concern. In this consists our hope.

Von Balthasar begins the fourth volume of his Theodrama with the book of the Apocalypse (TD4, the Action). He shows us that the victory is God's but that lies in the future. We are in the in-between times – the time of the great chaos and confusion. He quotes Adrienne Von Speyr who says:

> "Since all must be fulfilled, there must also be this momentary fulfillment of eternal pain (like a 'still' taken from a film), and of this too the saints must have knowledge."[3]

Our lives in this time are stills of the moment of God's pain, the pain of the one who gives birth to the new creation and the new earth – the transformed world. We are already a new creation in Christ by the power of the Holy Spirit (2 Cor 5:17) but what we are to be in the future we do not yet see. We come to know Christ who is risen from the dead and shows us in this our hope is not fake. For now, things might appear to be dark and the world a sad place, yet in this night we are not alone. God gives meaning to our suffering and with him truly tender is the night.

Our pain is God's pain. We wait in hope for his final victory when all this pain will cease. The end of the book of revelation captures this waiting in hope:

> I, Jesus, have sent my angel to attest these things to you for the sake of the churches. I am the sprig from the root of David and the bright star of the morning.
> The Spirit and the Bride say, 'Come!' Let everyone who listens answer, 'Come!' Then let all who are thirsty come: all who want it may have the water of life, and have it free. This is my solemn attestation to all who hear the prophecies in this book: if anyone adds anything to them, God will add to him every plague mentioned in the book; if anyone cuts anything out of the prophecies in this book, God will cut off his share of the tree of life and of the holy city, which are

[3] A. Von Speyr, Apokalypse (Einsiedeln, 1976) cited in TD4, p. 464.

described in this book.
The one who attests these things says:
I am indeed coming soon.
Amen; come, Lord Jesus.
May the grace of the Lord Jesus be with you all. Amen.

(Rev 21:16-21)

Conclusion

Beauty Will See the World

Albert Hammond wrote a song called 'Names, Tags, Numbers and Labels' (1974). In it he tells us how we classify each other and how we accept very often the labels others impose on us, but "when my name for you is beautiful your name for me is fool". We accept the negative things people say but if someone says we are beautiful we find it very hard to hear that voice. Albert Einstein once said that each person is a genius! He gave a little parable to emphasise this. In the parable, amongst others, is a fish and a monkey. If the teacher says to the monkey and his friends true intelligence consists in being able to climb trees, when the fish hears this he feels inadequate. John Lennon said in an interview in 1969 that every child is an artist until he's told he's not an artist.

In Dostoyevsky's novel, 'The Idiot' (1869), Ippolit says to Prince Myshkin: "Is it true, Prince, that you once said 'Beauty will save the world'". "Gentlemen" he (Ippolit) cried out loudly to everyone "the Prince maintains that beauty will save the world". Dostoyevsky portrayed Myshkin as a Christ-like person in our world and he is one seen as the idiot. Like Christ he is rejected by the world. The beauty of which the Prince speaks is the beauty of love, the love that heals and saves. I use Ps 8 to meditate on how God sees us and how in the end we pray to see ourselves. God sees us as beautiful as his children, as a mother and father see beauty in their new-born child. We are such children in God. God's name for us is beautiful.

Psalm 8 reads as follows:

For the choirmaster *On the … of Gath* Psalm Of David

> Yahweh our Lord,
> how majestic is your name throughout the world!

Whoever keeps singing of your majesty higher than the
heavens,
even through the mouths of children, or of babes in arms,
you make him a fortress, firm against your foes,
to subdue the enemy and the rebel.

I look up at your heavens, shaped by your fingers,
at the moon and the stars you set firm –
what are human beings that you spare a thought for them,
or the child of Adam that you care for him?

Yet you have made him little less than a god,
you have crowned him with glory and beauty,
made him lord of the works of your hands,
put all things under his feet,

sheep and cattle, all of them,
and even the wild beasts,
birds in the sky, fish in the sea,
when he makes his way across the ocean.

Yahweh our Lord,
how majestic your name throughout the world!

(Ps 8:1-9)

In the prayer those who pray it celebrate the awesome majesty of God the creator and also acknowledge that it is in this we find our dignity as human beings. The meaning of "Gath" or "Gittih" is far from certain. It probably refers to a musical instrument for those who sing the psalm. The psalm speaks of the grandeur and vastness of creation and God's special relationship with human beings who seem to form an insignificant part of this vast universe.

The psalm begins by praising Yahweh, the God who created all that is. The name of a person in the Semitic languages means one encounters the reality of the being of the person and his power (see R. Davidson, Le Message de la Bible, p. 30f). A name designates the person. The different names given to God try to help us encounter different aspects of his being. His name or names are modes of his Presence. He remains forever transcendent.

Creation reveals to us the greatness of the creator. I remember when the Hubble telescope went into space and began to send images back. It was a comedy of epic proportions on the part of scientists that Hubble got this far. Thankfully Hubble survived! The Universe was seen as vast and mysterious. It was once thought that the expansion of the universe would start to slow down. Instead it is accelerating and expanding. Since we do not know the name of the force that drives this expansion – we call it dark energy. Also scientists have found that there is a mass in the universe that encases what we call matter. Do we know what this is? No! So we call it dark matter. Every time we think we understand the universe it proves to be even more mysterious than we thought. Max Planck (1858-1947) was told when he began to study physics that he was wasting his time. All that there was to be known had already been discovered. When he studied black-body radiation he introduced a constant h – called the Planck constant. This led to the investigation of small particle physics, quantum mechanics, electrodynamics etc. The world of the small is mysterious and confusing. Richard Feynman, a Nobel laureate in physics, would joke: "People say science takes away from the beauty of the starts – mere globs of gas atoms. I, too, can see the stars on a desert night and feel them. But do I see less or more". Another time a student of his couldn't convince his mother of the beauty of physics. He asked Feynman as a favour to write to his mother. Feynman said sure. He wrote words to the effect "don't listen to your son! He talks a lot of rubbish. The only important thing is love…" It is the child-like wonder of a child that appreciates the wonder of all. To become a child again and be spontaneous and in love with all is a journey we embark on. Picasso described how he learned to paint as an adult, but when he saw his nephew paint with spontaneity and freedom, he said he had to learn again to paint as a child. This helps us understand what Jesus said: "I praise you, Father, Lord of heaven and earth, for hiding these things from the learned and clever and revealing them to little children" (Lk 10:21). Thérèse of Lisieux was the one who lived this. To the proud the world is a closed book, but to the eyes of a child all is wonder and love. St. Gregory of Nyssa said: "man, arrogant all that is, counts for nothing. He is dust, grass, vanity yet he is the one adopted by the God of the universe as a child…" (PG 44:1280).

The early Fathers of the Church spoke of the Macrocosmos and the Microcosmos. The Macrocosmos refers to the Universe – the Microcosmos refers to another universe, even more mysterious than the universe we see, that is the human person. I remember a comment by William Styron, the author of "Sophie's Choice". He said that we do not really know the human mind. It is as if we arrived on the shore, see a little sand but true knowledge of all that is lies in the great world beyond the seashore.

Blaise Pascal (1623-1662) wondered at the marvels of the universe. He was an extraordinary mathematician and scientist. One time he had an experience of God's love poured into his heart. He wrote: "Fire, God of Abraham, God of Isaac, God of Jacob, not of the philosophers and scholars…" and concluded by quoting Ps 119:16: "I will not forget thy word. Amen." In his Pensées he reflected on how the God of the universe loved us so much (Pensées, 119). He would also say that all the bodies of the universe, all the firmament, isn't worth anything compared to one single soul (Pensées, 793). True love is worth more than the movement of the stars. In the psalm man is called 'enosh' in Hebrew – this signifies the fragility of the human person. Yet this fragile being has been made a little less than God. In Genesis 1 we read that God gave this fragile being dominion over creation. Dominion here means care for. We read "… for dominion belongs to the Lord, and he rules over all creation" (Ps 22:28, Ps 103:19). He shares this dominion with human beings. We are his partners. In psalm 90:3 we read: "You turn us back to dust and say 'Turn back, you mortals'". This is the fragility of the partners of Yahweh. In Ps 8 we see Yahweh's love of his people. He delights in us and his dream is we be healed, and usher in a new creation. In Gen 1:26-29, we hear of God who made us, man and woman in his likeness. It is true that we have fallen from that image and defaced it, but in Ps 8 God sees us as we can be and are called to be. There is no negativity in the psalm. We are all embraced by God's love.

'How great is your name in all the world'. It is in God we live, and move and have our being (Acts 17:28). In praying Ps 8 we learn our dignity as God's beloved children. Many voices have distracted me from that place. I began the book by talking of Tillich's courage to accept acceptance (faith). In praying Ps 8 we enter the world of God's acceptance and love. This is what gives us the courage not to listen to the destructive voices but the voice of the one who cares, who believes and is eternally in love with us. We need to pray the psalm, be still, and in the silence allow the flame of love be kindled in our hearts.

Bibliography

Auden, W.H., *The Age of Anxiety* (New York: 1948)

Barth, Karl, *Anselm: Fides Quarens Intellectum* (London: 1960)

Barth, Karl, *Church Dogmatics* (Edinburgh: 1956-1975)

Barth, Karl, *The Epistle to the Romans* (In German: Der Romerbrief) (London: 1933)

Barth, Karl, *The Word of God and The Word of Man* (Gloucester, Mass: 1978)

George, Bernanos, *Diary of A Country Priest*, London, Boriswood, 1937

Brasnett, B., *The Suffering of the Impassible God* (London 1928)

Brueggemann, Walter, *The Message of the Psalms* (Minneapolis: 1984)
'From Hurt to Joy, From Death to Life' in *The Psalms and the Life of Faith* (Minneapolis: 1995)
'The Formfulness of Grief in *The Psalms and the Life of Faith* (Minneapolis: 1995)
Isaiah 40-66 (Louisville: 1998)
A Shape for Old Testament Theology I -Structure Legetimation - *Catholic Biblical Quarterly* -47 (1985) 28-46
A Shape for Old Testament Theology II - Embrace of Pain- *Catholic Biblical Quarterly* -47 (1985) 395-415
'Hopeful Imagination' (Philadelphia: 1986)

Dahood, M, *Psalms* (3 vols: Anchor Bible 16, 17,17a) (Gordon City, New York: 1966, 1968, 1970)

Davidson, Robert, *The Vitality of Worship: A Commentary on the Book of Psalms* (Edinburgh: 1998)
The Courage to Doubt (London: 1983)

Galot, J., *Dieu souffre-t-il?* (Paris: 1976)

Heschel, Abraham J, *Man's Quest for God*
(New York: 1954)
God in Search of Man: A Philosophy of Judaism
(New York: 1955)
'On Prayer: *Conservative Judaism, 25, No 1* (Fall, 1970) 1-14
The Prophets (New York: 1962)
Who is Man? (Stanford University Press, 1965)
The Insecurity of Freedom: Essays on Human Existence
(New York: 1966)
'No Religion is an Island' in *No Religion is an Island*
(Eds. Harold Kasimow and Byron L Sherwin, Maryknoll: 1991)
A Passion for Truth (Woodstock: 1995)

Jacquet, Louis, *Les Psaumes et le Coeur de l'Homme*, 3 Vols (Brussels: 1975-1979)

Julian of Norwich, *Revelation of Divine Love,* chapter 31.

Kuschel, Karl-Jose,f *Born Before All Time? The Dispute over Christ's Origin* (London: 1992)

Long, Stephen, *Saving Karl Barth: Von Balthasar's Preoccupation* (Minneapolis: 2014)

Martelet, G., *L'au-delà Retrouvé, Christologie des fins dernières* (Paris: 1974) p. 181-188.

Mays, James L, *The Lord Reigns: A Theological Handbook to the Psalms* (Louisville John Knox Press, 1994)
Psalms: Interpretation (Louisville: 1994)

McCann, J Clinton, *A Theological Introduction to the Book of Psalms: The Psalms as Torah* (Nashville: 1993)

Miller, P D, *Interpreting the Psalms* (Philadelphia, Fortress Press, 1986)
They Cried to the Lord: The Form and Theology of Biblical Prayer (Minneapolis: 1994)

Moltmann, Jürgen, *Theology of Hope* (London: 1961)

Moltmann, Jürgen, *The Crucified God* (London: 1973)

Moltmann, Jürgen, *Why am I a Christian?* in Experiences of God (London: 1980), 1-18

Moltmann, Jürgen, *The Trinity and the Kingdom: The Doctrine of God* (London: 1980)

Moltmann, Jürgen, *The Spirit of Life: A Universal Affirmation* (London: 2009)

Péguy, Charles, *La Porche du Mystère de la deuxième vertu,* 1911, in Oeuvres Poétiques complêtes (Paris: 1957) p. 527-670

Ravasi, Gianfranco, *Il Libro Dei Salmi* (3 Vols) (Bologna: 2002)

Rocchetta, Carlo, *Guarì Tutti i Malati* (Bologna: 2015)

Six, J.-F., *Itinéraire spirituel de Charles de Foucauld* (Paris: 1983)

Solzhenitsyn, Alexander, *We Never Make Mistakes: Two Short Novels* (contains Matryona's Home) (New York: 1971)

Steinbeck, John, *The Grapes of Wrath* (New York: 1939)

Steinbeck, John, *East of Eden* (New York: 1952)

Steinbeck, John, *The Log from the Sea of Cortez* (New York: 1951)

St. Thérèse of Lisieux, *Letters of Thérèse, vol II* (Washington: 1998)

Valensin, Auguste, *La Joie dans la Foi* (Paris: 1969)

Von Balthasar, Hans Urs, *First Glance at Adrienne Von Speyr* (San Francisco: 1981)

Von Balthasar, Hans Urs, *Heart of the World* (San Francisco: 1979

Von Balthasar, Hans Urs, *Plus Loin que la Mort*, Communio no. VI, 1 1981, p. 2-5

Von Balthasar, Hans Urs, *You Crown the Year* (San Francisco: 1989)

Von Balthasar, Hans Urs, *Love Alone is Credible* (New York: 1969)

Von Balthasar, Hans Urs, *Theology and Holiness,* Communio (Winter 1987) p. 341-350

Von Balthasar, Hans Urs, *Theological Aesthetics*, 7 vols, T. & T. Clark, 1982-1989 (GL in text)

– *Theodrama*, 5 vols, T. & T. Clark, 1990-1998 (TD in text)

– *Theologic*, 3 vols, T. & T. Clark, 2000-2005 (TL in text)

Von Balthasar, Hans Urs, *Mysterium Paschale* (Grand Rapids: 1993)

Von Balthasar, Hans Urs, *Explorations in Theology III, Creator Spirit* (San Francisco: 1993)

Von Balthasar, Hans Urs, *The Unknown Lying Beyond the Word* in Explorations in Theology III, Creator Spirit, p. 105-117

– *The Holy Spirit as Love, Explorations in Theology III*, Creator Spirit, p. 117-135

Von Speyr, Adrienne, *Isaias*, (Einsiedeln: 1958) p. 154f

Von Speyr, Adrienne, *Apokolypse* (Johannes) (Einsiedeln: 1977)

Von Speyr, Adrienne, *John, The Birth of the Church* (San Francisco: 1994)

Wright, N.T., *Paul and the Faithfulness of God* (London: 2013)

Wright, N.T., *Romans*, p. 393-770 in the New Interpreters' Bible, 10 (2002)

Printed in Great Britain
by Amazon

26388545R00076